MARCUS AND ASHLEY KUSI

EMOTIONAL AND SEXUAL

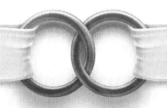

INTIMACY IN MARRIAGE

How to Connect or Reconnect
With Your Spouse, Grow Together,
and Strengthen Your Marriage

Publishing services provided by:

 **Archangel Ink**

ISBN-10: 0998729108
ISBN-13: 978-0998729107

Your FREE Gift

As a special THANK YOU for purchasing this book, we have created a printable worksheet to help you implement what you will learn during the 30-Day and 12-Month Intimacy Challenge.

Visit www.ourpeacefulfamily.com/intimacyworksheet to get your copy of this free fill-in-the-blanks worksheet.

JOIN OUR EMAIL COMMUNITY

To receive email updates about future books, courses, workshops, and more, visit the website below to join our book fan community today.

http://www.ourpeacefulfamily.com/bookfan

Dedication

To all the couples that are committed to making their marriages the best they can be.

CONTENTS

INTRODUCTION

You have most likely picked up this book because you can see your marriage could use improvement in the intimacy department.

Maybe you have a hard time connecting with your spouse emotionally, sexually, intellectually, physically, or spiritually. You feel something is missing in your marriage, you are slowly drifting apart, and you want to rediscover that connection you once had together. You might even be afraid of intimacy because you don't want to get hurt.

Just like many couples, we used to feel the same way. Over time we grew apart and we missed the deep and meaningful connection we had in the beginning. To be honest, we were terrified about waking up one day to see ourselves living like strangers.

Once we admitted that something was missing in our marriage, we decided to recreate that intimate connection.

Why?

Because we did not want a monotonous marriage that lacked intimacy, excitement, and fulfillment. As you may already know, unresolved intimacy issues can lead to feeling distant, lonely, rejected, unappreciated, boredom, frustration, and could result in divorce.

Can a small change transform a level of intimacy in your marriage?

In our case, we came up with a plan and took action. This simple plan, which helped us to transform and strengthen intimacy in our marriage, is the most *essential* thing you can do to rekindle intimacy in your marriage.

We now feel connected emotionally, physically, sexually, intellectually, spiritually, and much more. In addition, we spend more quality time together, and we have more meaningful and deeper conversations.

As you just read, intimacy in our marriage has improved a lot, and we want to help you experience it in your marriage too.

For your marriage to flourish, you and your spouse have to feel intimately connected to each other in all areas of your marriage. You both have to feel fulfilled and happy to experience intimacy on many levels. As you already know, all marriages can benefit from enhancing their intimacy. This book is just the place to start.

We've all heard about married couples that have filed for divorce because they have grown apart, feel like roommates, or don't share any interests anymore. However, we believe that if a couple decides to enhance intimacy in all aspects of their marriage, they can recreate the connection that is missing.

You can have the happy, healthy and fulfilling marriage you both dreamed about when you said, "I Do." You can turn that missing connection and desire into an advantage. Instead of getting divorced, start pursuing your spouse. Better yet, learn how to reconnect with your spouse.

You see, intimacy is so much more than what happens between the sheets. Effective communication, trust, and a safe environment also play a huge role in developing intimacy and helping you to deeply understand your spouse.

The fact is connection is an intrinsic part of our lives as human beings; especially as a married couple. There are thousands of studies about human connection and the lack thereof. One such study by Dr. John T. Cacioppo, compared individuals who had high levels of social interaction versus those who were more isolated in their daily lives.

The study found that: our social connections impact our lives in every single way. Our physical health, cognition, our ability to get a good sleep, and reduce the levels of stress or inflammation in our bodies (the main factor of autoimmune diseases) is dependent on these bonds. This is why our closest relationship of marriage should be one of the most powerful and strongest connections we have. If our marriages suffer, we suffer.

As marriage coaches, we know through our experience, conversations, and research that there are many couples who are missing this deep connection in their marriage. That's why we wrote this book. We want to help couples like you learn how to connect or reconnect in every way throughout your marriage. This book is for the couple who knows something is missing, as well as the couple who want to rekindle and take intimacy in their marriage from good to great.

What are the deepest needs that are not being met in your relationship? Can you appreciate your spouse's presence in your marriage? Are you willing to start by looking inward and working on yourself? Are you able to trust your spouse? Are you at least open to trying? If you are, then we welcome you to begin this process of learning how to truly connect with your spouse so that you can have healthy intimacy in all areas of your marriage.

We suggest you start with a marriage check-up. Find out the state of intimacy in the different areas of your marriage. Ask each other, "On a scale of one-to-ten, ten being the best, how strong of a connection do you feel in this area of our marriage?" Find out how connected you both feel in these key areas: emotionally, as friends, intellectually, spiritually, relationally as a parent or spouse, financially, socially, sexually and physically.

Finding out where each of you are, will help you to discover the areas that may need more attention as we dive deeper into this book. Knowing where you are weak is the first step in trying to rekindle and strengthen intimacy in your marriage.

In addition, to keep your intimacy strong, create a special distraction-free time in your calendars to spend together. *Spending time connecting every day* is the most essential thing that has made a huge difference, transformed and strengthened intimacy in our marriage.

As we mentioned, we will show you how you can intentionally do the same for your marriage. If you and your spouse spend time deliberately connecting every day for a year, you will be amazed at the results. You will feel emotionally connected, build trust, and experience a satisfying sex life. In addition, you will build a safe haven that will allow you and your spouse to talk about your feelings, dreams, fears, struggles and desires. Now imagine what would happen if you do nothing about what's missing in your marriage today. Most likely you will be in the same place ten years from now, or worse.

Today is the best time to learn how to strengthen intimacy in your marriage, and this is the book to guide you.

Chapter 1
EMOTIONAL INTIMACY & FRIENDSHIP

"The best and most beautiful things in the world cannot be seen or even touched. They must be felt with the heart."

– Helen Keller

Emotional intimacy is an amazing part of marriage. Honestly, it is one of the best ways to keep that fire burning in your relationship. Being connected emotionally helps you grow together throughout your everyday life, and in your marriage.

From our experience, there are many ways to connect emotionally. However, the root of that connection is sharing a part of yourself with your spouse and feeling that they are getting to know you intimately. In the same way, when your spouse shares himself with you, and you feel that you have come to know your spouse, you are connecting. Cultivating a deeper knowledge of each other will prevent you from becoming bored and growing apart in your marriage.

An intimate connection cannot happen every time you speak to each other because deep conversations take time. You should also be somewhat rested so that you can be present with your spouse. In our experience, when this does happen, it leaves you with feelings of satisfaction, connection, and thankfulness. Have you ever had a deep conversation with someone and felt like you could stay up and talk to them all night? Like that conversation was more important than sleep? A conversation where you are totally focused on that person, knowing them, understanding their point of view, empathizing with them and sharing yourself to be known?

When I think back to our first "date" night, I remember having a conversation at three o'clock in the morning that lasted until six. It was that conversation that impacted both of our decisions to really get to know one another and gave us a feeling that something beautiful could happen. We felt heard, connected and respected in our different views. We were real.
– Ashley

A marriage without emotional intimacy is unfulfilling. When you are missing something in your relationship, you may naturally start to look elsewhere to fulfill that need. You may turn to a friendship, hobby, or even another relationship. To protect against this, you must learn to be emotionally vulnerable with your spouse.

Connection with another person is something humans crave. Our need to connect is as basic as our need for food and water. Sociologists suggest that when our social bonds have been cut or are in danger of being lost, we humans will be grievously affected because we are impacted so immensely by our social environment. If these bonds are severed we can experience more than a metaphorical broken heart; there may be real physical pain. Losing these bonds in childhood can cause learning difficulties and can have a negative impact on a person's health (www.scientificamerican.com). Isn't that fascinating to think about? Our social connection, or lack thereof, can be felt physically. A broken heart when that connection is severed, the heart melting feeling when you are falling in love, or that uneasy knot in your stomach when something just isn't right. This is why having a marriage bond that you both feel intimately connected in every way is so integral to your marriage's overall health.

We can think of many stories of people who have money and fame, but that isn't enough. They are miserable because they have no one share it with. These connections are important for your health and the state of your marriage. Cacioppo said, "One of the major functions of the human brain is to enable skilled social interactions and permit stable and satisfying social relationships. (www.psychologytoday. com)." Your own brain is hardwired to seek these connections and thrive off of them. Connecting with your spouse is why you chose to get married in the first place, isn't it? You wanted to find someone that you could share your life with. You wanted to have someone by your side through everything that life could throw your way. You wanted someone to laugh with, and someone to hold you when you need a good cry. You chose to commit to this personal and intimate relationship of marriage, to share in this powerful connection.

So, how can you be there for your spouse on an emotionally intimate level? By getting to know your spouse. Even if you have been married for twenty years, there is always something new to learn about your spouse. You are always growing and changing. Your interests, priorities, and opinions change over time. Communicate with each other what is on your mind, what you are struggling with, what you are excited about, what you are anxious or worried about. Share with them what you are learning, how you are growing and what your goals are. Let your spouse view the world through your eyes, and try to see it through theirs too. Your spouse will not be the same person you married, they will evolve through their life, as you should.

Recently Ashley's youngest brother was in an accident and was paralyzed. The first month we were not sure if he was going to make it. During that time, I had to be a shoulder for Ashley to cry on, listen to her empathetically while she expressed her fears, and her struggles with me. I felt her pain and emotions even though I was not directly affected as much as she was. I felt her tears. – Marcus

Emotionally supporting each other will go a long way toward nourishing that closeness between the two of you. Being there for each other when one of you is upset and comforting one another. Being there to listen, being a shoulder to cry on, and giving advice when desired. Likewise, being there to laugh together, share exciting news, dream about your future goals and the life you are planning together will also strengthen your emotional intimacy. Emotionally mature couples care for each other deeply. They are empathetic and want each other to be fulfilled in every area of life. A strong emotional intimacy makes for a great physical intimacy as well.

HOW TO COMMUNICATE AND EXPRESS YOUR FEELINGS WITH YOUR SPOUSE

As a husband, I initially could not communicate my feelings to Ashley when we first got married because I was terrified. I wanted to keep my struggles to myself, so I did not appear "weak" to her. I found it hard to express my struggles and feelings.

My perception was a man must always be "strong." Even if he feels weak, he must never show it, especially to a woman. A man doesn't cry, right? Guess what, it's not true. My perception of what it meant to be a man and to be strong was wrong. Emotions and struggles is part of what makes us human.

Keeping everything inside just made it harder to share my feelings and struggles with Ashley. Being able to express my feelings has made me a better man, husband, and father. I have become a better communicator simply because I can share my feelings and struggles without feeling "weak," and I don't have to appear "tough" and guarded with my own wife. – Marcus

By sharing your struggles with your spouse, they will be able to see a part of you that has been hidden. They will recognize you are also a human being, filled with deep emotions, who is honest and sincere with them. Your spouse will be better able to relate and empathize with you. To be honest, it took us a while to learn how to communicate and express our feelings with each other. Since we both started opening that part of ourselves up to each other, our marriage has become stronger, more intimate and fulfilling.

It is easy to get stuck in your head with the what-ifs:

» What if her response hurts my self-esteem and confidence?

» What if she judges me and starts to think less of me?

» What if he makes fun of me in his head without me knowing?

» What if she loses the respect she has for me?

» What if he gets sad, mad, or even angry?

» What if her reaction or response is a very negative one?

» What if sharing my true feelings causes more fights?

» What if she thinks I am weak?

» What if I end up crying?

» What if I feel ashamed?

» What if I feel rejected?

» What if my feelings get crushed?

» What if I am not able to fully express my feelings so she can understand them well?

» What if she does not care to know my true feelings?

» What if he is uncomfortable talking about it?

» What if she cries?

Those are a lot of the what-if scenarios I had in my head, consciously and subconsciously. All of these what-ifs were the main reason I found it hard to share my feelings and struggles with Ashley. However, I also believe it is very important for my wife to know what I am going through, especially the feelings I experience, whether good, bad, mixed, or uncertain. It is integral to our intimacy and our communication that I share my struggles with her. – Marcus

Your spouse should be the closest person to you. He is the one you go to bed with every night. She is the one you wake up to every morning. They are the one you chose out of the millions of people in the world to spend the rest of your life with. Not being able to communicate your feelings and struggles with them just does not make sense. In addition, you will be missing a deep connection that greatly impacts the intimacy in your marriage.

You see, being vulnerable makes me feel like I am appearing "weak," and for most men, that's the worst feeling to have. To truly connect and be intimate with Ashley, I had to bare my soul and hold nothing back. I had to open up. I had to believe that the what-ifs were just living inside my head and were likely to be unreal. After all, they were the reason why I was afraid to communicate my feelings, struggles to be open and vulnerable to my wife. – Marcus

You might also have multiple what-ifs, but do not let that stop you from communicating and expressing your feelings with your spouse.

FOUR AMAZING TOOLS THAT WORKED FOR US (AND COULD WORK FOR YOU TOO!)

First, we pondered about our what-ifs, and came up with the list shared above. What are your what-ifs? Do you hesitate to share your feelings and struggles with your spouse? What makes it difficult for you to communicate and express those struggles with your spouse? Why are you keeping your emotions to yourself?

Get a piece of paper or your journal and write them down. Just writing out what you are afraid of is an important exercise that will help you identify the conscious and subconscious reasons you are not communicating your feelings with your spouse. Now, think about what will happen if your what-ifs are not true? What difference do you see? How much easier would it be to communicate and express your feelings?

Second, we chose to believe wholeheartedly that our spouse always had the best interest for us, even when it didn't feel true. "She would never do something to purposely hurt me." This belief made a huge impact on us. In fact, we intentionally had to say this mantra to ourselves several times until it became a part of our mindset.

I felt disconnected to Ashley whenever I perceived she did not have my best interests in mind. I felt hurt, distant, and worried. All those negative feelings changed the moment I started to believe she had my best interest at heart. – Marcus

Third, we talked a lot about anything and everything, just like we did when we were dating. We had deep, meaningful conversations about, our marriage, dreams, goals, faith, and life. These conversations made it easier to discuss our emotions, which in turn made it easier for us to communicate our feelings and struggles to each other without feeling judged.

As we got older and had children, we realized we were not having these deep conversations anymore. So, we scheduled a minimum of thirty minutes to have meaningful conversations every day. Having this type of face-to-face communication, like you would if you were trying to learn everything you could about a person, certainly helps in many ways. It helps you feel relaxed, open-minded, and comfortable enough to share your feelings and struggles. Read the chapter about intellectual intimacy for a list of conversation starters.

Fourth, identifying our exact feelings was very important so we could effectively communicate and express them with each other. We had to learn to identify the feelings we were having, be they good, bad, mixed or uncertain, making them easier to articulate. Whenever we communicated our emotions to each other, we used a lot of I-statements.

An I-statement follows this structure: I feel (describe the feeling or word for the emotion) when (cause of the feeling, such as events, triggers, moments, or whatever happened that led to the emotion).

For example: "I feel worried and stressed when we do not have enough money for the month." Another example is: "I feel shy and uncomfortable whenever we talk about our sex life."

By using I-statements, I could express my emotions to Ashley without making her feel like I was blaming her for my emotions or that she had control over them. It also subconsciously made me feel in control and responsible for my feelings. - Marcus

Sometimes, you might not be able to identify the actual feeling. Instead, just write down what you believe caused it, and how long it lasted. Then you can discuss your notes with your spouse, and maybe they can help you identify what the feelings were. We often had to discuss our emotions this way and figure out how to deal with them together.

With the good feelings like when one of us got a promotion, it was always easier to communicate and express them. It was the negative and unsure feelings that were harder to communicate.

As soon as you have a negative emotion as a reaction to something your spouse said or did, try to share it with your spouse so you can both deal with it together. If you don't, over time, the negative emotions will compound, and eventually lead to resentment, hurt feelings, and emotional distance from your spouse. Putting off communicating about negative emotions can easily lead to heated arguments and unnecessary fights. That is why it is so important to use effective communication when dealing with your emotions.

BENEFITS OF COMMUNICATING AND EXPRESSING YOUR FEELINGS WITH YOUR SPOUSE

Now, I just tell Ashley as I am experiencing an emotion, or struggling with something, because of how open we are about sharing them with each other. We feel safe doing it and do not judge each other. We listen empathetically and provide sincere and honest feedback. When Ashley needs more time to give me a better response or process specific feelings or struggles I share with her, we just schedule time to talk later that day. – Marcus

The feedback you will receive will not always be easy to hear. It may make you feel disappointed and want to hold back. However, we believe listening to your spouse open their heart up to you is the best thing to hear. From our experience, even though it hurts sometimes, we always feel relieved afterward and are better for it in the long run. So we try our best to not get angry, react, argue, or yell while we have our discussion. We stay calm and listen quietly so we can share more of what we want each other to understand.

Being able to communicate and express my feelings with Ashley makes me feel like I have a giant weight lifted off my shoulders. I am not as stressed as I used to be. I can tell her how I feel even when it's a scary emotion or difficult struggle. I don't have to keep all my feelings inside, something that used to suck the energy out of me. I am also able to provide feedback when Ashley shares her feelings with me. I feel we influence each other's lives in a positive way, thereby strengthening our emotional intimacy. – Marcus

On occasions when you feel resentment for your spouse for no obvious reason, it is most likely because you feel they do not understand your feelings about something, or that they are taking your feelings for granted. It could also be that you are projecting negative feelings you have for your boss at work, experienced with the cashier during checkout, or the driver who cut you off on your way home onto your spouse. Although your spouse was not present when these feelings started, you might resent them for their lack of understanding.

Your ability to communicate your feelings with your spouse is essential to have fulfilling intimacy in your marriage. As humans, we all want to be heard and understood for who we are. So why not develop the courage to express yourself to your spouse? Don't be stuck and frustrated with your feelings. Instead of keeping your lonely thoughts to yourself, share them with your spouse. Express them with the person you have the closest and most intimate relationship with. Tell your spouse about your deepest feelings, fears, struggles, and joys.

Now comes the best part. Because we can share our feelings, struggles, and be vulnerable without fearing that we are being judged, our sex life has improved tremendously. Sex is now better and more satisfying because we feel intimately connected emotionally, physically, and spiritually.

The quality of your sex life and sexual intimacy depend on how safe you both feel with each other. The slightest appearance of resentment can make sex unsatisfying.

Sex starts in the mind. Talk about your sex lives. It could be an uncomfortable conversation at first, but it could also be a conversation that takes your sexual intimacy to new heights. These conversations can make you feel uncomfortable, hurt, and self-conscious, but it is the same conversation that can take intimacy in your marriage to another level. So get ready to dive in and have an intimate conversation with your spouse about sex.

One thing we do is to rate our sex life on a scale of 1 to 10, with 10 being the best. That might sound scary to you, and it does involve some practice. We try to do this on a weekly basis to make sure both of our sexual needs are being met. More on this subject later in the chapter about sexual intimacy.

PRACTICAL WAYS FOR CONNECTING EMOTIONALLY WITH YOUR SPOUSE

* **Find out how each of you feels connected emotionally to help recreate that missing intimacy.** What does emotional intimacy feel like to you? What about your spouse? Have a conversation and really think about this. Be open-minded to what your spouse has to offer and try not to get defensive. Remember, empathetic listening is key when you have conversations with your spouse.

* **Get rid of your resentments and hurt feelings.** Get everything out on the table, so you don't have anything holding you back. This will take empathetic listening and trust. Be open-minded as you listen to where your spouse is

coming from. Be respectful when you explain things, and take responsibility for your actions and emotions. Share things you might have been nervous to bring up before. If there are a lot of issues that you both need to go over to get on the same page and have a fresh start, do this in increments. It is okay to take your time as long as you do this together.

We had an argument recently about how I was feeling rejected and that I wasn't getting the attention and connection I needed. I wasn't even sure what was at the root. I had a lot going on in my personal life that had triggered some things for me, and I finally realized it was that familiar feeling of rejection that I had dealt with during our first year of marriage because of my past.

Marcus verbalized that he understood me by saying, "I understand you feel rejected by me and that we haven't connected because I have been busy and I am going to try to do better tomorrow." Then he added that the rejection was my emotion that I needed to take responsibility for because he was not rejecting me.

That got me thinking and helped me realize what was at the root of these old feelings that had come up. It helped when he verbalized it for me, promised to do better and then does just that. Then I can think about what I can do to better this situation, so we don't end up here again. – Ashley

   * **Be open, honest, and willing to meet your spouse part way.** Compromising is a part of any relationship. Trust is the glue in a marriage. Without trust, a marriage will crumble.

Being honest with each other, being willing to meet your spouse where they are, and giving each other a safe place to vent your feelings and frustrations without fearing it will incite an argument is a must for emotional intimacy. Learn to apologize instead of blaming each other.

* **Listen with empathy and affection.** There is no place for defensiveness when you are trying to grow. Use empathetic listening to try to understand where your spouse is coming from. Why did he do what he did? What was she thinking or trying to accomplish? Believe she had the best intentions and ask about it while explaining how whatever was said or done made you feel. Remember to pay attention and try to see things from their perspective.

* **Share your weaknesses and struggles with your spouse.** Reach out and discuss your fears, concerns, and insecurities. Be emotionally vulnerable. Let your spouse know if you need advice to solve this issue together or if you just want a listening ear. This can get mixed up really easily; it happens all the time in our marriage. Make it clear to your spouse: "I need you to just sympathize with me right now," or, "I need some help solving this problem." That way, your spouse knows exactly what you need and how to help.

Being vulnerable with your spouse is integral to helping build the bond between you both. Marriage should be your safe place to find help, solace, and comfort. You both have the power to create this safe place for yourselves. Read the chapter about fear of intimacy to learn how to create a safe haven for your marriage.

* **Be there for your spouse.** Whether they need a shoulder to cry on, help to find a solution, or just you being there with them to support them through the difficult times you face individually or as a couple.

* **Be grateful and show appreciation.** Tell your spouse what you love about them, why you appreciate them. By showing how you appreciate your spouse's efforts, you are staving off the resentment. It is easy to get caught up in life and take for granted the ways your spouse contributes. A simple, "Thank you for remembering to do the dishes," or "Thank you for just being the amazing person you are," can do wonders when it is genuine and heartfelt. More on appreciating your spouse later.

* **Set some goals together.** Emotional intimacy blossoms through communication in sharing your dreams, your hopes, and your life together. Planning for your future, whether immediate or farther off, helps guide you both on working together to achieve these goals. Growing together strengthens your emotional bond and improves your communication.

Sharing your personal goals along the way helps you to know when the other partner may need encouragement. It helps you to know how big a deal it is when your spouse hits their goal. This is just one more way to bring you both the emotional intimacy you desire.

* Reminisce on the past you have shared, everything you have gone through together, and how far you have come. We typically do this around special dates, anniversaries, or the New Year. We take the time to reminisce at least every couple of months, because when we face any difficulty life throws at us, we can always look back and see how we made it through our past difficult times together. We have that history to rely on and remember, as do you. Thinking about the past can encourage you to keep going and press on together. It can be very enlightening to see just how far you have come together.

* **Cheer each other on.** Share your successes together, as well as the struggles. Be each other's cheerleader. You are there to help keep your spouse accountable and to celebrate your successes, whether this means you are on the sidelines while your spouse is playing their favorite sport, or sitting with them while they sell their wares at a farmer's market. Be there for each other and have your spouse's back.

* **Observe and appreciate the good qualities of your spouse as a person, a spouse, and as a parent.** Think about all the good things your spouse does, how blessed you are to have them in your life, and how happy you are they choose you every single day. This is an especially important exercise to do when you are feeling negatively about your spouse. Remind yourself of the good that your spouse has brought to your life.

* **Have a conversation.** Share your thoughts and feelings. These conversations could be about anything from politics, work, business, acquaintances, anything that gets you both sharing what you each think. It can be fun to see where your opinions and feelings differ and where they align.

Another great conversation previously mentioned in the introduction, is a marriage check-up. Take the time to talk about how fulfilled you both are in the different aspects of your marriage and how you can make it better.

*Let your spouse know you trust their abilities and show respect.** Do not be afraid to verbally let your spouse know that you trust them and their abilities. Let them know you respect them with your words and your actions. If someone tells you they respect you but their actions say otherwise, that disrupts any trust you have built together and erodes your intimacy. Here is the takeaway: your words and actions must line up.

* **Don't let your past experiences prevent you from being completely vulnerable with your spouse.** As humans, it is normal to build walls and go on the defensive when we are hurt. When you get married, it is your responsibility to lower these walls and let your spouse inside.

These walls can form for many reasons: your parents' relationship (or lack thereof), your own relationships (exes), abuse suffered or witnessed, disappointment in role models, and other baggage. We are not able to pick the house we grew up in, the parents we were born to, or unsafe and violent circumstances we had to endure. However, we can decide to move on from those and create a healthy and safe environment for our marriage and family. By hanging on to these past violations, you can derail your marriage and hold it back from its full potential.

Remember your spouse is not the same person as your mother, father, ex, or abuser. Your spouse is the person you fell in love with and chose to marry. Do you not trust them for legitimate reasons, or because you are afraid in light of your prior experiences? Your fear of intimacy can be stopping you from experiencing a deeper intimacy with your spouse. Read the chapter on fear of intimacy to discover how you can overcome it.

Please understand we are not saying that you should blindly give your spouse all your trust if he is not trustworthy because of addictions, abuse, or habitual lying. These are deeper issues that will require counseling. Divorce should be an option if it is because of the more dangerous issue of abuse and untreated addiction. If this is your situation, please seek help from a professional immediately and get to safety.

* **Cook together.** Choosing a meal together, shopping for ingredients, coming home and cooking together, enjoying the meal and cleaning up together afterward can turn everyday tasks into a fun way to connect emotionally. You are sharing your life tasks, communicating in different ways, and enjoying each other's company. You are learning about each other, and that is one of the best ways to become emotionally intimate.

* **Recreate your first date.** Have fun with it. It may not be the same place, but get creative. Your spouse will appreciate your efforts.

* **Go stargazing.** Watch the stars next to a fire. Enjoy the sunrise with a hot cup of coffee, or watch the sun setting with a glass of wine. Snuggle close, and just be together in that moment. Talk if you want, or just enjoy each other's presence along this journey of life you chose to do together.

* **Write your spouse a love letter.** Receiving a piece of paper upon which your spouse took the time to write, or type, all their feelings and everything they appreciate about you and your efforts can mean a lot. A love letter can be especially handy for the spouse that has trouble articulating exactly how they feel out loud. Surprise your spouse with this gift of transparency. If you are not sure where to start, we wrote an article just for you. You can read it at www.ourpeacefulfamily.com/loveletter.

You have to be able to fully express yourself in order to have a fulfilling marriage. To be honest, sharing your shortcomings is never easy but it is necessary if you want to be yourself and not a stranger to your spouse. Tell the truth about how you feel, whether you are discouraged, embarrassed, excited, scared, or overwhelmed.

For example, if you are the breadwinner for your family but hate your job, be honest and share your pain with your spouse. Explain why you feel that way and what you think could help you with this situation. Discuss and work together to create a plan that will help you to solve this issue together. Your spouse might not like to hear it at first because they might be worried about how the bills will be paid if your paychecks stop coming in. However, because your job impacts your overall happiness as a person and your marriage, your spouse should be willing to help you find work you love.

Sharing my feelings and struggles allowed me to free my mind and have more energy. – Marcus

From our experience, the more you share your feelings, articulate your struggles, and show vulnerability with your spouse, the easier it becomes. The fear you used to have will eventually go away too because you will have created that safe place with your spouse. Just like any skill, the more you practice, the better you become. The goal is to create a relationship dynamic where the two of you can be completely honest and open with each other without feeling judged.

Sometimes, one of you may feel connected, and the other does not. So be honest, and voice your feelings. Why do you not feel connected to your spouse? What is missing that you are seeking? How can your spouse help you find that missing connection you desire? Connecting, for some people, is the little things like hugs, kisses, letting them know you appreciate them or having a conversation is what helps them feel connected. For others, it is the steamy, passionate lovemaking, visiting a new city, regular date nights, or long discussions. We are all unique individuals and we all feel connected through different ways.

FRIENDSHIP

*"Friendship is born at that moment when one person says
to another: 'What! You too? I thought I was the only one."*

– C.S. Lewis

Friendship in marriage is a form of emotional intimacy; it is so important that it merits mentioning by itself. Emotional connection in a marriage helps solidify that bond and creates the most intimate friendship with your spouse. The word friend is defined as, "[A] person attached to another by feelings of affection or personal regard...supporter." (www. dictionary.com) When you think about your relationship with your spouse, do you feel affection and support from them? Do you think that you give them your affection and support? Ask your spouse and see if they agree.

Cultivating friendship with your spouse can be a great experience for both of you. You can celebrate all the things you have in common together, learn from each other's strengths while supporting each other's weakness. One of our favorite ways to grow our friendship is to do something where we can talk and laugh together. We love getting active and learning a new sport, game or activity. It refreshes us.

Author Elie Wiesel once said, "Friendship marks a life even more deeply than love. Love risks degenerating into obsession, friendship is never anything but sharing." Love isn't the only thing that will help a marriage survive. Friendship is required for your marriage to thrive and be fulfilling. When you see an elderly couple still deeply in love, what stands out to you about them? Their enduring friendship? Their ability to have fun and laugh together? Their deep-rooted compassion for each other?

When you think about friendship, in most instances, it is the trust between two people. It is the honesty, desire, and willingness to share your success, failures, struggles, new discoveries and parts of yourself with your friend. In our marriage, I see Ashley as that friend. She is the one I can talk to about anything and everything without feeling judged. She provides me with constructive feedback. She is honest with me about the ideas I have whether they are challenge worthy or too risky. This is how I see our friendship. I value her feedback and opinions so much that, I don't make any decision that affects both of us without talking to her to get her take on whatever it is. – Marcus

We hate to be the bearer of bad news, but the truth is your stereotypical physical attractiveness will fade away. Your skin will become loose and wrinkled. You may lose your hair, or grow it in places that aren't as flattering. You may gain weight. Physical attraction will not last without that emotional closeness. Think back to when you first met your spouse and your initial physical attraction. Compare it to the attraction you feel for them now. How is it different?

When I think back to my feelings about Marcus when we started dating, when we first got married, and now, I can see how our love has evolved. The love I have for Marcus has matured through the years. The first year, I honestly felt my heart

would burst and that I couldn't possibly love him anymore. I have learned since then that there are many stages of love. The love we have now is much more deep-rooted within our souls. I look forward to seeing how our love changes in the years to come. I was not as attracted to him as physically in the beginning as I am now. Or maybe, just like with our love, that physical attraction deepened from the shallow lust to being drawn to him as a whole person. The more I get to know him, the more attracted I become – Ashley

If you feel your friendship or any area of your marriage is lacking, we encourage you to look inward first. See if there is something you need to change for yourself to make your life better. Could it possibly be a bad habit you have? After you identify the root, or if you need help, talk to your spouse. Express to your spouse that you feel that your relationship needs more attention in a certain area and you need help. Your relationship can't work if only one of you is making an effort. It will take both of you to cultivate this friendship into what you both desire for your marriage.

Around our fifth wedding anniversary, I started getting that feeling of routine when it came to our relationship, both inside and outside of the bedroom. I felt like something was lacking. It wasn't the physical aspect so much as it was a lack of connection emotionally. I tried thinking about what I needed Marcus to do. Maybe if he surprised me more. Maybe if we went on more dates. Maybe if he... But then I realized my problem was inward.

Even though my happiness should be encouraged by my husband, it is ultimately in my hands and must not be dependent on anyone else. I had to figure out what was at the root of this feeling that something was missing. I had to take a step back and think about what my ideal marriage looks like and how ours is different. I realized I needed more connection emotionally. We needed to grow our friendship and focus on sharing ourselves with each other more.

We communicated about this and carved out more time to spend one on one to just talk and connect. We found other ways that we cover later in the book like working together, dreaming together, and laughing together. – Ashley

As William Shakespeare once wrote, "A friend is one that knows you as you are, understands where you have been, accepts what you have become, and still, gently allows you to grow." There can be so much freedom in marriage when you build strong connections, so you both feel secure. Your marriage can become a relationship in which you respect each other's boundaries, encourage each other to grow in healthy ways, and accept each other as you are. Growing more intimately connected in every way as your love matures is the ideal marriage. Friendship is an integral part of that intimacy.

WAYS TO BUILD AN INTIMATE FRIENDSHIP WITH YOUR SPOUSE

* **Do an activity together that takes you out of your comfort zone.** This can be a lot of fun. Teaching each other something you enjoy, or letting your spouse share their hobbies with you can be a great way to bond. Growth will not happen unless you move past your comfort zones and are willing to put yourself out there.

* **Learn something new together.** This goes along with what was mentioned above, but this time, it should be new to both of you. Whether it is a new cuisine, restaurant, vacation spot, sport, activity or anything that the two of you have never tried together, do it!

* **Volunteer together.** Giving back while spending time together is a great bonding experience. Make some meals and hand them out to the homeless, or volunteer at a shelter. You both have the opportunity to do something selfless while growing your friendship and connecting.

* **Drink coffee.** Have a coffee date and talk, laugh and enjoy each other's company with no distractions. As simple as it sounds, a trip to the local coffee shop or teahouse, sitting side-by-side and enjoying an hour of good conversation can do wonders for your emotional intimacy. Communication is a huge part of friendship.

* **Go see a comedian and laugh together.** Laughing builds trust, and trust is the glue that holds a marriage together. Laughing with your spouse, having a great time together,

not worrying about anything or anyone can be a great way to enhance your intimacy. Be silly, and goof around, laugh and share jokes with your spouse. How long has it been since you had a good belly laugh together? Pull up a funny YouTube video, or steal one of our ideas: hide in the closet and jump out at your spouse in the dark. (Just be prepared for reflexes!)

* **Dream together.** Talk about what your dream job is, or your dream house. I know we mentioned dreaming together before, but it is just that important. When you dream with your best friend and spouse about how you want your life to be, you are sharing a part of your core with them. Bonding in this way will create a strong connection.

* **Be honest.** Be honest with each other. Create a safe place without judgment, and be willing to give and receive constructive feedback. Your spouse should be your safe place, and you should be theirs. Your spouse is also there to help give you those constructive critiques when you need to hear them. You can start by sitting down together and having an open mind. Ask your spouse one thing you could do better, what you are doing well at, and how you have improved since your last conversation.

* **Shop together.** Whether it is grocery shopping or a department store, sharing these types of experiences and making it fun together will enhance your friendship and intimacy.

* **Go to an event together.** Watch a game, see a show, or attend a party. Get out of the house, dress up like you did on

your first date, and enjoy sharing this experience with your spouse.

   * Share. Recommend things to your spouse that you know they are interested in, even if you are not stimulated by it, such as blog articles, resources, news, movies, etc.

   * Be there when your spouse needs you. It can be that simple. A huge part of emotional intimacy and friendship in your marriage is to simply be there for your spouse when they need you. Be there for each other to rely on whenever there's a job loss, a bad health report, or an unexpected disappointment. Be there in the hard times as well as the good times. Be there to celebrate and congratulate each other when you make it through, when you achieve your goals, and when you win.

There have been many challenging times in our marriage because life has thrown us so many curve balls, from job loss to health issues. Marcus was there through it all when I needed a shoulder to cry on. He gave me encouragement to keep on going, the frank truth and healthy critiques when I needed them. He was there to celebrate when of all the hard work paid off, and I hit my goal.

I have several autoimmune diseases. One of them is called Hashimotos Thyroiditis. This means my own immune system is attacking my organs. Marcus was there to comfort me when I finally got diagnosed; when I was a crying mess. He was there to give me the tough-love answer of this being our new reality. He didn't complain that my new lifestyle meant we had to spend more on food so that I could get the proper nutrients and heal my body. He was there when my test results came back not as I had wanted. He was there when I finally found out I was in remission.

Seeing his face and hearing him tell me how proud he was of me for reaching this goal was so worth all of the struggles. Knowing he was there with me through it all made it that much more special. I know I can rely on him when everything is crashing around us. I know he will be my rock. – Ashley

* **Vacation or getaway together.** There is no better way to build a friendship than adventure and relaxation. Plan your next vacation or getaway together.

* **Take notice in what your spouse is doing.** It shows your interest.

* **Create something together.** Working on a project together will help you to connect emotionally. This could be a business or a piece of furniture, creating a child, a home, a home improvement project, a piece of art, or a charity. Working as a team on something tangible is a great outlet and way of bringing the two of you closer. When you work on something with your spouse that you both care about, you can see your partner in a different light.

* **Work out together.** Sweating together is a unique way to grow closer together. No, not just in the bedroom. Work on a project together, enter a race or play a sport that gets you both active. Have fun together, work as a team, and burn some calories!

* Create routines and rituals. Going to bed at the same time, waking up together, planning your day while drinking coffee in bed or having breakfast with each other is something little you can add to your daily routine. Adding these daily points of connection will strengthen your intimacy. Yearly rituals like setting goals for the New Year can be a great way to grow together and stay on the same page. We do a yearly "7 days of sex" challenge where we try to have sex for seven consecutive days. We set individual goals for the year as well as our marriage, family, spiritual, financial and business together. One other thing we do is pick a book that we will both read or re-read, and discuss what we each learned from it.

For more information about the "7 days of sex" challenge, visit the resources page at the end of this book.

* Pick different face-to-face activities. Try different activities like talking over coffee or playing a game. Then choose side-by-side activities like building something, working on something together, or whatever you both are interested in. Create your own board game together. Mix up these activities so that you are creating variety in the ways you connect together.

* Play an instrument together. Go to a music shop and try out the array of instruments. If neither of you are particularly musically inclined, go to a concert or symphony together.

* Get outside together. Go for a hike and have a picnic at your destination.

QUESTIONS TO ASK YOURSELF AND YOUR SPOUSE

» Are there any secrets you have kept from me?

» How do you/I feel most connected in our friendship?

» When do you feel emotionally connected and intimate with each other?

» What can we both do to deepen our intimacy in friendship?

» What is one thing we can do this week to make our emotional intimacy stronger?

GET TO KNOW YOUR SPOUSE AND YOURSELF

How do you feel connected emotionally? Write down 5 ways with specific examples, so your spouse knows how best to connect with you. Then make it a point to do at least one thing your spouse listed every day.

Spouse A

1.

2.

3.

4.

5.

Spouse B

1.

2.

3.

4.

5.

Chapter 2

INTELLECTUAL INTIMACY

"If you want to know where your heart is, look where your mind goes when it wanders."

– Unknown

Connecting intellectually with your spouse can be achieved in different ways. The main goal is to find your mutual intellectual interests. Intellectual connection keeps your mind busy. It is what makes you want to talk to your spouse for hours and hours. For your marriage to really flourish, you have to have intellectual intimacy.

Your marriage should be a safe place where you can talk to your spouse about anything and everything under the sun. It is a chance to have your mind challenged and worldview widened. This kind of chemistry between you helps solidify friendship with your spouse. Intellectual connection brings that deep intimacy between the two of you because you are bonding on a more meaningful level, which is imperative to your marriage.

We all want to be known and loved for who we are as people. Having your spouse connect with you through intellectual conversation helps expand your mind, increases your respect, and strengthens your bond. Therefore, it is important to find those shared pursuits between you both.

As you may already know, your brain is your biggest sex organ, so put it to work! It is completely logical to deduce that by having a strong intellectual intimacy with your spouse, your sex life will be that much more amazing and satisfying because they go hand-in-hand.

We enjoy connecting intellectually through deep conversations, especially when our opinions differ and we try to see things from each other's point of view. Learning from each other can help you feel intimately connected. We love to come up with thought-provoking questions to ask each other. Usually, these conversations happen organically as we share with each other the new things we are discovering about ourselves, our desires, and all the things we get excited about.

We humans are happiest and most fulfilled in relationships when we can be challenged to expand our knowledge and worldview. According to The New York Times, researchers indicate that our natural search to deepen our understanding and enhance our experiences can be attributed to something called "self-expansion." The more our spouse challenges us to expand intellectually and improve our minds, the more connected, attracted, and satisfied we feel with them (Tara Parker-Pope). Your spouse should help inspire you to learn more about the things you feel innately attracted to.

Talk about your intellectual goals. Talk about what you want to learn more about, where you want to be in five years, what you are learning about now, and what you are working on in your self-development. Find the commonalities. You may be interested in different physical things, but they can have shared meaning.

Intellectual connection is one of my favorite ways to connect. I love when we have those deep conversations that make me feel like we could talk all night. These conversations help me feel connected and fulfilled because I feel like I am getting to know Marcus' innermost thoughts. I am also able to share parts of myself that rarely get to come out in our day-to-day life. Feeling like I get to know him better in different lights each time gives me something to look forward to, and it keeps the spark alive.
– Ashley

It is easy to think we know everything about our spouse after being with them for any length of time. These intellectual conversations help remind us that we are always growing and changing, so there is always something new to learn about each other. Connecting in this way keeps that excitement alive between the two of you.

In addition, intellectual intimacy cultivates a part of us that needs constant challenge and attention, our brains. Our brains are always active, even when we sleep. To think that we can have a life-long marriage and not need to give our intellect attention is neglectful. Connecting intellectually nourishes your marriage, your friendship, and you as an individual.

One specific way we practice intellectual connection is through running a small business together. We balance each other's weaknesses and strengths. Finding ways to work together has opened up parts of our relationship to connections we hadn't even anticipated. Making decisions about the direction of the business together, and then pursuing those hand-in-hand brings us closer together because we get to work as a team. Connecting on an intellectual level and incorporating our dreams for life together has shown us parts of each other we hadn't known about before. It isn't always easy; if it were, it wouldn't be a challenge.

Working on a small business together with my husband, I learned to trust him more. He understands so much more about online business and takes some risks that I used to get so nervous about. Through running our business and pursuing what we are passionate about together, I do not worry like I used to. We make all the decisions together, and when I don't feel comfortable with something, he respects that, and we don't do it.

When I do not understand all the technical needs for the business, such as software, I trust him to make the right decisions. Have we made mistakes? Yes, we are far from perfect. Has he disappointed me or broken that trust? No. I feel so much respect from connecting with Marcus intellectually because he truly values my opinion. I see him take action with my advice and it makes me feel cherished by him. – Ashley

Another way we connect intellectually is navigating through life. We talk about difficulties and issues we are having. We share our struggles and make it clear to each other if we just need emotional support, or if we need advice.

Voicing your needs is imperative in all aspects of marriage, but this seems to be a common miscommunication between couples. It is truly an amazing feeling to be able to lean against your best friend, and talk to them about the challenges you face and be able to collaborate and find a solution. Even if you do not feel like you are best friends with your spouse at this point in your marriage, if you continually work on connecting in these different ways, you will become closer than you ever thought possible.

After I was diagnosed with Hashimotos Thyroiditis, I had to learn how to heal my body through food. I had to cut out all grains, dairy, and sugar. It was a few months before the holidays, and all I could think about were the food I couldn't have. I was sad thinking about all the traditional family cookie recipes that I wouldn't be able to pass on to my girls. I was having a pity party. I realized how emotionally connected to food I had been.

Marcus saw how upset I was, and he said, "If you want to be healthy and live a long life, then this is what has to happen. Find other things you can have." He gave me the cold, hard truth. This was my life now. I had to grieve this loss, as crazy as that sounds. He helped bring the most important factor to my attention, and that was my health. I wanted to be able to live as long as I could with a healthy mind and body. I didn't want to have to rely on him or my children to take care of me. I didn't want to be a burden.

So, bit by bit I cut these things out. Grains and sugar first. I found many new recipes that turned out delicious. I substituted almond flour, coconut flour and cassava flour for regular flour. Then when I had to cut out almonds because we discovered my daughter and I are allergic to them, it was not as big of a deal. I found a substitute that works for everyone without sacrificing the taste.

Marcus was there for me to vent to when I needed him, but he also gave me the realistic and sound advice I needed to hear. He connected with me logically and used that intellectual connection to help me see the goal while I was in emotional distress. He has been willing to try new foods out with me, supportive of the budget changes needed to live this lifestyle, and understanding of the fact that we can't really eat out anywhere now. – Ashley

Intellectual connection helps you to better understand your spouse. We can have more compassion with someone we feel a bond with. Connecting intellectually with your spouse helps you to know them like no other person can. It guides you to understand where they are coming from, their intentions, and how best to communicate with them. Intellectual intimacy cultivates friendship, solidifies the bond in your marriage, encourages growth, and challenges your mind.

I feel intellectually connected to Ashley when we have thought-provoking conversations that center around our

projects, marriage, beliefs, challenges, and goals. We had a conversation about divorce rates. We looked at the statistics and decided we didn't want to be part of them. We discussed why we thought marriages ended in a divorce, and then what we could do to stay happy and fulfilled in our marriage. We made a plan together, and I really enjoyed seeing how committed Ashley was to our marriage, as well as seeing her point of view on this issue. We took action together and check-in consistently.

Another example is a project I am working on. Soccer is one of the many passions I pursue, and naturally, I wanted to start a soccer blog. I came up with five different names for the blog. I asked Ashley her opinions on them, and she helped me come up with the perfect one. By seeking her opinions and starting that conversation about why she likes certain domain names and why not others, it helps me connect with her on my level. – Marcus

Find out where your connection is lacking, and then ask your spouse how they feel most connected to you intellectually. How do you feel most challenged, and want to talk to your spouse for hours and hours? Not sure where to start? Think about conversations you have had with your spouse where you felt fulfilled. What were you talking about? What was it that you enjoyed the most? Try starting conversations about those bigger ideas and thought-provoking questions that have to do with life, spirituality, beliefs, art, politics, history, priorities, productivity, and so on. Find that conversation that makes you feel like you want to dig deeper.

THOUGHT-PROVOKING CONVERSATION STARTERS

Finding some conversation starters can help you both when you feel like you have run out of things to talk about. Here are a several questions that we have found helpful:

» What challenges have you had in your life that you are grateful for?

» How would you like to start your ideal morning?

» What is the hardest truth about love you learned the hard way?

» What is the hardest truth about life you learned the hard way?

» What is the hardest truth about our marriage you learned the hard way?

» What is the one moment that made you fall in love with me?

» Have you ever felt rejected by me? When did it happen?

» Have you ever resented me? When did it happen?

» What have you been interested in lately?

» What are you are afraid to talk about with me because you are worried that my answer might hurt your feelings?

» In your opinion, what is the one thing we have argued about the most in the past ninety days? Why, and how can we resolve it?

» When you talk about me with someone, do you have positive, negative, or neutral things to say? What about when you think about me?

» What can I do to make sure you feel safe with me?

» What goal would you like us to accomplish together by the end of this year?

» Do you feel I am there for you when you need me? What can I do to show you I am there for you?

» What is your favorite memory of our wedding day and night?

» When do you feel respected and disrespected by me?

» Which married couple do you look up to the most and why?

» What is one thing about me that you discovered, after we got married, that you love? One thing you dislike?

» What is something I do that makes you feel loved the most and unloved?

» What is one worry you have had about our money and finances in the past thirty days?

» How best can I help you around the house?

» What is the best investment we should make or do this year for our marriage?

» What are you most excited about this year?

» What could I do to make you feel more appreciated?

» How would you describe our marriage in three words?

» What do you think is better than amazing sex?

» What is the one unanswered question you have?

» What were the highest and lowest points of your life? What about our marriage?

» What is your first memory of me? Describe it in detail.

» How can we make our marriage affair proof?

» How can we build trust with each other?

» How can we communicate better?

» What does your ideal career look like?

» What does your ideal life look like? What does your house look like, and where is it located? How many children do you have? How much time do you spend with me one on one? With each child?

» How many family activities do you want to have going on each week/month?

» How often do you prefer to eat out?

» How often do you want to cook at home?

» What do you want to do for fun?

» What do you want the atmosphere in your home to feel like?

» What does the perfect marriage look like to you? Explain in detail.

» Have you ever saved someone's life? Has anyone ever saved your life?

» What person (or people) had the most impact on your life and how?

» What do you do to get yourself in a better mood when you are not feeling so great?

» What do you want to be remembered for?

» What book has influenced your life the most?

» What would you do if I changed my religious beliefs?

» How do you feel about supporting family members financially? What if one or more of your parents needed to be taken care of? Would they live with you?

» What makes you attracted to me - physically, emotionally, intellectually, spiritually?

» What makes you feel connected to me?

» What brings you the most joy in our marriage?

» What are you dreading in life right now?

» What have you struggled with your entire life? Does anyone know about it? Why do you think you struggle with it? Have you overcome it? How did you overcome it?

» What are the most important things you have learned from your parents?

» If one of you had to be on life support, would you want to continue to be kept alive? What if you had no brain activity? What if you were paralyzed or needed to remain on life support to stay alive for the rest of your life? What if you were in a coma?

» How do you want to be buried/celebrated and where? These are extremely tough and emotional conversations, but they are needed. A recent family experience has brought this subject up for us, and we decided it is best to know what each other's wishes are rather than not knowing and having to choose at that time.

If you are looking for more questions to discuss together, join our book fan email community for updates on our next book about conversation starters for couples at www.ourpeacefulfamily.com/bookfan.

Think about those times when something happens, or you learn something about yourself, and you have that overwhelming urge to share it with your spouse. Find where you're intellectually compatible, and spend time delving deep into each other's knowledge, opinions, and experiences. Once you discover where you have shared intellectual interests, make a plan to keep that connection alive. Make a point to continue growing that connection, and continue to explore this uncharted new world as a couple. Carve out time every day that is solely devoted to connecting intellectually.

WAYS TO CONNECT INTELLECTUALLY WITH YOUR SPOUSE

* **Give your spouse your undivided attention.** This may seem like common sense, but this is getting harder to do with so many of the distractions in today's world. As much as technology has improved our lives, if you are not careful, the

same technology could deprive you of the intimacy you desire in your marriage by replacing your conversation and face-to-face connection. One of the simplest yet most effective ways to start improving intimacy in your marriage is by turning off the electronic devices like phones, television and video games when you are together. By doing this simple thing, you will be able to start connecting with each other more effectively.

* **Pick a book to read together.** We usually pick one book to read or re-read together each year. We read it individually and then discuss it together. It is interesting to see the different takeaways we each get from the same book.

* **Set goals together.** Sit down at a coffee shop and have a conversation about your goals for this year or this month. Set goals for your money, health, relationship satisfaction, education, politics, business, anything and everything that affects your life. Or if you are like us and have younger children that make it hard to leave the house, wait for them to fall asleep and make a cup of tea or share some wine and cuddle up on the couch together. Have a conversation that forces you to push your boundaries and come up with ideas. We mention goals a lot because a marriage without goals will essentially lead to you growing apart.

One of the things we started discussing this year was the possibility of moving to another country. There were a few countries we liked, and after some discussions, New Zealand was our top choice. It started out as mentioning it a few times, and then grew into sharing articles with each other about the country. We talked about the pros and the cons. We made the decision to stay in the United States, but if we ever decided to leave, that is where we would want to move. It was fun to imagine a life there and discuss this possibility together. Have you and your spouse ever considered a move to another country or state?

* **Plan something fun together.** Go on a vacation, weekend trip, or day trip. We try to plan a couple fun things every month, even if they involve our children. They don't have to cost money. It can be hiking, bowling, visiting museums, going to the lake or ocean, traveling to see family, fishing, window-shopping, or latte sipping. Whatever is fun for both of you.

* **Teach your spouse something.** Learning from each other and sharing your knowledge is a great way to bond intellectually.

* **Take a class together.** Art class, cooking class, business class, brewery or chocolate making class. See what resources are available in your city, and take advantage of them.

* **Discuss career options.** Are you both happy where you are with your careers? Where would you like to be in three years? Are there any projects at work you are stuck on, or issues that your spouse can help give insight to in finding a solution?

* **Supporting your spouse's health struggles, whether they are physical, emotional or mental.** Research alternative solutions that could help and have a conversation; share notes.

* **Brainstorming with your spouse about life.** Starting a business, places to visit, bucket list for your marriage. How do you and your spouse view the world, politics, religion, choice, rights, etc.? Exchange thoughts on a topic or issue. Find a topic you know you both love to discuss or a pose a new question.

* **Share your daily wins.** Your spouse is your partner in life. Do not forget to share with them the things that go your way during the day. Did you get that promotion? Share it. Did you complete a personal goal? Share it. Did that recipe finally turn out right? Share it!

* **Play a game that makes you think.** Scrabble, Upwords, Clue, puzzles, and card games. This is a fun way to use your brain and bond together. For more game ideas visit www. ourpeacefulfamily.com/games.

* **Cultivate your own interests.** Keeping your own identity and growing individually will help you both to be able to grow your intimacy.

* **Engage in each other's interests.** It may help you remember why you fell in love with them in the first place.

* **Be financially intimate.** Budgeting together, setting up a financial plan so you are agreeing on where and how much you spend is key to having a fully intimate relationship with your spouse. Money plays a huge role in our lives, whether we want to admit it or not. Two people going their own separate ways with money can lead to a lot of conflict. Sit down together and make a short-term plan for a monthly budget, and a yearly budget. Finally, plan for bigger goals such as retirement, buying a house, investing, starting a business, and donating to charities. You will both become more financially intimate, even if you decide not to share bank accounts. As you work toward these goals on the same team, you will open up channels of communication you never knew existed before.

QUESTIONS TO ASK YOURSELF AND YOUR SPOUSE

» How do you each feel the most connected to each other intellectually?

» What is one thing you can do this week to deepen that intimacy?

A FUN INTELLECTUAL INTIMACY EXERCISE TO DO WITH YOUR SPOUSE

Using the questions below, find three to five different ways to pose each question. An example would be, "What is your biggest challenge in our marriage?"

» What is your biggest challenge about X?

» What do you think about X?

» How do you feel about X?

» How did you X?

GET TO KNOW YOUR SPOUSE AND YOURSELF

How do you feel connected intellectually? Write down 5 ways with specific examples, so your spouse knows how best to connect with you. Then make it a point to do at least one thing your spouse listed every day.

Spouse A

    1.

    2.

    3.

    4.

    5.

Spouse B

    1.

    2.

    3.

    4.

    5.

Chapter 3
SPIRITUAL INTIMACY

*"Giving someone a piece of your soul is better than giving
a piece of your heart. Because souls are eternal."*

– Helen Boswell

Having a spiritual connection with your spouse will help both of you come together in an area of life that is inherent. Even if you don't share the same belief system (we don't), it is possible to find things you have in common.

We realized that many religions and personal belief systems share a lot of similarities, though they use different words to describe the same thing. If one of you believes in prayer, while the other believes in sending good intentions out into the universe, you can do those things together.

If one of you wants to talk about character lessons or parables from the Bible, Torah, Quran or another spiritually enlightening book with the other, then go for it. Just because you may or may not believe the same way, it doesn't mean you cannot take the good from each of your spiritual beliefs to share together as you connect. How have beliefs impacted your way of thinking? How have your beliefs spoken to you about your life? Talk about what it means to you and how your beliefs speak to you.

Many belief systems incorporate meditation in one form or another. So if you both practice meditation together, you can connect on a spiritual level. You could sit quietly together in the same room, or hold hands as you focus on your breathing and verbalizing your intentions. Even if you choose to meditate separately, you can have a conversation about any new revelations, progress or struggles you discover during meditation. Share this part of your life with your spouse in any way that you can.

You can always have a conversation about where you are on your spiritual journey, what you are learning and what questions you have. Being able to converse about spiritual matters with your spouse, without feeling judged, can be one of the best ways to feel safe in your relationship and become spiritually intimate. When you talk about your beliefs and your innermost questions, you open up a side of yourself that is so deeply rooted in who you are. It encourages being open-minded and pushes each other's boundaries to be exposed to a new worldview while empathetically listening to your spouse.

Both Marcus and I believe we are all spiritual beings. We believe in a bigger force or energy, but we each have different names for this. Marcus believes in a God, while I like to think of this entity as the universe, Gaia, or Mother Earth. We can find a place to come together and explain to each other why we believe differently; why one of us is hesitant to explore one way or the other.

I believe one of the most important things we do, because we believe so differently, is to keep each other in the loop with what we are learning, questioning, and exploring. That way, we don't wake up one morning and not know who the other person is spiritually. The other important thing that we do is respect each other's beliefs. – Ashley

Let's be frank, a difference in fundamental spiritual belief systems can scare a lot of people. However, if you think about it, even if both spouses share the same religion, they can differ in their interpretation of sacred text, in their philosophy, and with what laws should be followed versus what laws are just suggestions.

When we were first married, we both shared the same belief system. A few years into our marriage, Ashley started seriously questioning things and slowly lost her belief in the same things as me. Even though she had kept me in the loop the whole time she was questioning things, it still came as a shock to me. I had always believed a husband and wife should have the same belief system, and now my worldview was being put to the test. We talked about it, and we still believed in the same core values, such as treating each other how we want to be treated.

This made me realize that our spiritual journeys can change over time. However, as long as we can be open with each other, stay on the same page, be respectful of our differences and holidays we wish to observe; then a spiritual belief difference

in marriage can still work, and we can remain spiritually connected. – Marcus

The truth is, we can all find things in common with our spouse spiritually. You are different from your spouse in many ways, and yet you find things in common. You married a completely different person than yourself, and your spirituality is no exception. Your spiritual intimacy should be no different. What makes spiritual intimacy one of the deepest connections you have with your spouse is because it goes to the core of who you are. Spiritual connection gives you and your spouse a sense of unity.

WAYS TO ENHANCE SPIRITUAL CONNECTION WITH YOUR SPOUSE

* Set a time to have a one on one conversation with your spouse about each of your spiritual journey's and how you have come to the place you are now. You can even take a walk together as you discuss this topic. What does the word "spiritual" mean to both of you? What are some big questions you have about your faith? What are some questions you have about your spouse's spiritual beliefs? What makes you uncomfortable about your faith or your spouse's faith? Do you feel respected spiritually by your spouse? This discussion is a win-win, not an argument or debate. It should be you discovering who your spouse is spiritually, and why they believe, or do not believe, the way they do.

One thing that is important to us with our spirituality (and our whole marriage) is the boundaries that we have created. Because we have different beliefs, we have to talk about what exploration would make each other feel uncomfortable. We have to discuss things to make sure we are in unity and not hurting one or the other with what we say, or how we treat certain things one of us may see as spiritually significant. It involves a lot of respect, communication, and open-mindedness, especially since we have children.

* **Appreciate your differences.** Find out where your journeys have been different, and where your beliefs differ. We are uniquely different from our spouse in many ways. Discover where your beliefs diverge from your spouse's. These conversations can be very intriguing and aid your spiritual connection. Feeling like you are unearthing something new from your spouse and knowing them more deeply strengthens your spiritual intimacy. This conversation also has the potential to become emotional and in-depth, so make sure your phone and other distractions are put away. Focus on understanding your spouse from their point of view and explain yourself in a way they can empathize with you.

* **Talk about what you share in common spiritually.** Find ways you can connect together through these commonalities. Where do your spiritual practices merge? Finding spiritual activities that you share in common with your spouse brings you closer together. That may just mean having conversations

about your journeys and checking in with each other once in a while.

* **Explain to each other where you feel the closest to whatever higher power you believe in.** Is it in the woods? Is it in a church, temple, or mosque? Find a way to encourage each other to find the time, and go to that place they feel the deepest connection to their higher power.

Obviously, it helps if both of you get onto the same page when it comes to where you are at spiritually. Don't be afraid to ask questions, but make sure this is a judgment-free-zone, so both of you feel safe enough to open up. You have to be able to trust your spouse, respect their different opinions and beliefs. You are in this marriage for the long haul. If you want a truly fulfilling marriage, then you need to try to connect with your spouse on every level. Sometimes it takes baby steps, and that's okay.

* **Spiritual sex.** From our experience, spiritual intimacy can happen in many ways. Conversation and sharing the common practices of your belief system does not have to be the only way. Have you ever experienced complete spiritual connection during sex? Being completely connected on another deeper level, like a meditative state, feeling like you are not sure where you end and your spouse begins? Being intimate physically as well as spiritually can be a world changing experience. Of course, we will talk more about physical intimacy later in this book. For now, it is important to know there is such an experience as spiritual sex.

* **Find out where you are on your spiritual journey.** When it comes to spiritual beliefs, some questions don't have answers, and that's okay. Connecting with each other spiritually can be a challenging for some couples and second nature for others. That's why it is important to ask yourself questions and know where you are on your spiritual journey, where you want to be and what you want to learn. The important thing is asking the question. *Knowing where you are on your journey is really the first step you should take in connecting with your spouse spiritually.*

* **Keep each other in the loop.** Just as any area of our life, our spirituality evolves as we grow. Remember to keep each other updated every once in a while, with where you both are at, how some of your views may have changed, or evolved. You, your spouse, or both of you may change religions as we have experienced in our marriage, or simply come to a different understanding and philosophy of your shared spiritual beliefs.

* **Pray together or pray for your spouse**: Calling on the higher power(s) you believe in, verbalizing your intentions, sending love and light, or whatever prayer means for each of you.

* **Talk about the history of your beliefs, or any specific religion**: Learning the roots of your own religion, and others, can help you understand humanity better, not just your spouse. As humans, we tend to fear what we do not know. Educating yourself about other belief systems can take away that fear and aid you in your relationships, your marriage, and beyond.

* **Mediate together.** As mentioned before, meditation can be done in many ways. Sitting silently together or separately, verbalizing intentions, holding hands, and breathing deeply, or whatever works for the two of you.

* **Share the character lessons you are each learning from your sacred text.** Whether you believe in the Bible, Torah, Quran or something else, there are character lessons that you can discuss. Even if you are agnostic and do not have any sacred text, there are themes such as the golden rule (treating others the way you wish to be treated) that we can all glean some wisdom from.

* **Celebrate holidays that bring your together.** You have created your own unique family by getting married, and you get to create whatever new traditions you and your spouse desire. You can choose to celebrate or not to celebrate. You can take the good and leave the bad, and a whole new world will open up.

You can create and mold holidays to fit where you both are in your lives. Learning the roots of holidays has opened up so many new traditions for us, as well as finding ideas on Pinterest. Have fun with this one. Just because something has always been done one way doesn't mean you can't try another way. Construct the holiday experience that fits the family the two of you created by getting married. If this seems too much of a shock to one or both of you, try changing one thing, or adding one new tradition at a time.

* **Go to religious services together.** If one or both of you attend religious services, such as weekly or monthly gatherings at church, bible study, temple or somewhere, then plan some days to go together. You have to talk to each other. Communicate why this is important to you, ask your spouse if they are willing to come with you every week, or occasionally. Even if your spouse does not accompany you because that is the boundary they have set, you can have a conversation about what spoke to you and how you can apply this in your life.

* **Do a devotional, or some sort of character-centered book together.** Choose a religious book, a self-development book, or a book centered on an area of your life or marriage that you both want to improve. Having your spouse learn with you and be able to talk about what you are reading and gleaning from the same book can give you insights through each other's eyes. Working together to improve an area of your life or marriage aids you in strengthening spiritual intimacy.

While there are many ways to connect spiritually with your spouse, find the ways that work for your relationship because every marriage is unique. What works for one marriage, might not work for another; there is no one-size-fits-all method.

Dr. Brene Brown sums up intimacy best, "I define connection as the energy that exists between people when they feel seen, heard, and valued; when they can give and receive without judgment; and when they derive sustenance and strength from the relationship." Spiritual connection is an essential part of the intimacy in marriage because it is such a huge part of who we are as humans.

QUESTIONS TO ASK YOURSELF AND YOUR SPOUSE TO DEVELOP SPIRITUAL INTIMACY

» How do you feel the most spiritually connected?

» How do you feel spiritually connected with me?

» What can we both do to feel more connected to each other spiritually? Be specific.

GET TO KNOW YOUR SPOUSE AND YOURSELF

How do you feel connected spiritually? Write down 5 ways with specific examples, so your spouse knows how best to connect with you. Then make it a point to do at least one thing your spouse listed every day.

Spouse A

1.

2.

3.

4.

5.

Spouse B

1.

2.

3.

4.

5.

Chapter 4

RELATIONAL CONNECTIONS

"You have half our gifts. I the other. Together we make a whole. Together we are much more powerful."

– Joss Stirling

There are many different types of relational connection within a marriage. What we want to focus on in this section is your relationship as a husband or wife, as parents, and keeping that romance alive. After you get married, it is easy to get caught up in your new titles of wife/husband and forget that you are an individual. Conversely, it can be hard moving away from only having to think of yourself to now including another person into your decisions. Finding that balance for each of you being yourselves as individuals and as husband/wife can be your first challenge in your marriage. Adding parenthood to that balancing act can create even more confusion, stress, and friction.

We have all heard, or maybe experienced, that after a while, those butterfly feelings of love toward your spouse will dissipate. We asked ourselves, why did that spark have to go? How could we turn that spark into a blazing ember or full-on house fire? We have come to the conclusion that so many couples believe that initial spark will last without doing anything to feed that fire. A lot of couples let that deep connection and excitement they once had fade away, and then move on to the next relationship. However, in marriage, walking away is not that easy.

In order to keep that spark alive and well within your marriage, you have to keep feeding that flame. How do you feed that ember? Through connection and pursuing your spouse. Through being intentional about how you grow in all the different areas of your marriage. Your marriage must always be a top priority.

WAYS TO ENHANCE RELATIONAL INTIMACY IN YOUR MARRIAGE

* **Find your role in your marriage.** What do you expect of your spouse and what do they expect of you to do or be in your marriage? How do you view a husband or wife's role? What do you feel comfortable doing and what does your spouse feel comfortable performing? Many individuals have an expectation of what marriage looks like, and wrongly assume their spouse has the same understanding. But you have to verbalize these expectations and get on the same page to move forward in your marriage. Understanding each other's role is essential for connecting to your fullest potential.

After getting married, it almost felt like a power struggle within myself. I was a wife now, and yet I was still me. All these expectations of what being a wife really meant were swirling in my head. I knew I did not want to mold into the person I thought Marcus wanted me to be and lose who I was. I did not want to wake up one day twenty years from now and not know who I was. – Ashley

After you have a good understanding of each of your roles as husband or wife, you can focus on connecting as individuals and as a couple while your marriage evolves.

* **Make sure your cup is full**. You cannot give what you do not have. Taking the time to do things as an individual, within reason, will help you feel replenished and help you be able to give more to your relationship. Grow as a person. It can be very hard for some people to take time for themselves; others find it difficult to prioritize their marriage over their own personal time. As with all aspects of life, it is about finding the balance. Give your spouse time to do the things he or she loves doing and be thankful they can be themselves.

Soccer is one of my passions. Anything related to soccer gets my blood pumping and makes me excited. I play pick up soccer whenever I can because it is a time when I get to do the sport I love and not worry about anything else. It is my outlet. After I get some time to myself and play soccer, I feel replenished and am able to be a better person, husband, and father. – Marcus

* **Verbalize your appreciation for your spouse.** Think about your relationship overall. What are some things you really admire and appreciate about your spouse? These could be personality traits, sacrifices made, acts of service, or whatever you love about them. Tell them. Your spouse may

not know how much something they've done means to you. Hearing appreciation from your spouse feels pretty amazing. It feels good to be recognized by someone you love for doing everyday things, such as cooking dinner. It is a way of saying, "I see you, and I appreciate you. I love you. Thank you for being you." Let them hear you speaking positively of them in public too. One simple thing you can do every day is to thank your spouse for one thing before you go to bed.

I remember in the first year of our marriage, whenever Marcus would thank me for doing the dishes or cleaning the house, I was surprised because these were my jobs. I assumed this was just expected of me to do my part of the housework or whatever it was. Of course, I felt appreciated at the same time, and that made me want to tell him I was thankful for his efforts in return. This has helped carry us through all the changes in our life and has kept us connected. – Ashley

Verbalizing your thankfulness to your spouse helps stave off resentment and releases stress. Furthermore, you feel appreciated that your efforts are recognized. We can't stress enough how important showing appreciation is after becoming parents. Imagine your spouse has spent the whole day at home with the children, picking up the same mess over and over again, and the house still a wreck when you come home. You have basically two possible responses:

1. *Thank you, honey, for taking care of the kids all day. I know it isn't easy.*

   Or

2. *Why is the house such a mess? You've been home all day. The least you could do is pick up!*

The first choice encourages the cohesiveness of your marriage and your intimate connection because your spouse feels loved, encouraged, safe and not judged. The second choice, even if you only think it, can lead to disconnect and resentment, adding further stress to your marriage.

　* **Find balance.** Another aspect of marriage that many couples will experience is parenthood, adding yet another title to your life: self, husband/wife and now mom/dad. Whether you are trying to balance your life as a husband or wife, or as parents, it is imperative to find what works for your unique relationship. Not getting too busy and disconnected, but making time to just be yourself, to just be a husband/wife, and to just be a parent. Life is about experiences. The job that wants you to work sixty hours a week with that great salary won't be there on your death bed offering you loving words, but your family will.

　Before I was married, I played soccer four times a week. After I got married, my relationship with my wife became the priority and soccer went to once a week, then even less as I became a father. Finding the time to balance one of the things I love to do and be fully present in whatever I am doing has been world-changing. When I am with my wife, my attention is on her, my phone is away. When I am spending time with my daughters, they have my full attention to dress up and be their nutcracker, play hide and seek, or just sit close and snuggle with them while we watch Daniel Tiger together. I don't work more than fifty hours a week because I know my relationship and connection with my wife and daughters will suffer if I do. Finding the balance is difficult. I had to make a choice: Would I rather work more and make more money, or spend that time building my relationships and having experiences with my wife and daughters? Which was more important to me? – Marcus

* **Surprise your spouse.** Give something positive that your spouse isn't expecting. Whether you do the dishes so your spouse will find a clean and empty sink when it's his turn to do the dishes, or bring home her favorite beverage. Create a romantic gift basket full of her favorite goodies. The surprises don't have to be huge and complicated to have the impact you are looking for. If you have the means, surprise each other with hotel tickets for a night, a weekend trip, a gift on a normal day, or flowers. You could even take the day off and plan an adventure. The surprises can be as grand a gesture as you want, but simple acts of service can go a long way.

* **Be present**. Seeing your spouse in a new light can be refreshing and help you fall even more in love. Watching your husband let your daughter paint his nails and play dress up can show you a different side to him you never knew about. Seeing your wife breastfeed your child is a uniquely beautiful experience. This is part of your marriage connection. Having those moments when you are present and just observing your spouse as they parent can make you feel appreciative, loving, and connected with them. Even if you don't have children,

being completely present in the moments when you are together talking, grocery shopping, walking, or holding hands while driving will enrich the intimacy in your marriage.

After we delivered our first daughter, I became so enmeshed in being a mother that it was easy to just roll over snuggling my tiny newborn and forget that I was also a woman and wife. I learned to be intentional about saving energy to be a wife. That included having conversations that didn't just revolve around our day-to-day life; it also included sex. Finding that balance and reminding myself I am more than just a mom, I am still a wife and still myself, was so integral to our marriage. Balancing time to be mom, wife, and to do things for myself helped us stay connected. In addition, it helped me to be even better at my different roles. – Ashley

Of course, in your parental relationship, it is important to remember that a lot of times there is no right or wrong way of doing things. There is only your way and your spouse's way. It's okay if those ways are different; those different parenting styles could even be highly beneficial for your children.

* **Schedule sex.** Yes, sometimes sex needs to be on the calendar. Our lives go through busy periods, especially when we have kids. Sex needs to be a priority to help keep you physically and sexually connected. More on this topic in chapter six.

* **Date your spouse.** Always make time for just the two of you to talk and connect. Go out, stay in, do whatever works for your situation. Never stop pursuing your spouse.

Going out to dinner is not really an option for us because of Ashley's food allergies and diet restrictions. We also have two toddlers, so finding time to date each other looks very different than it once did for us. We still schedule time to go to a teahouse together or spend some time with just the two of us whenever possible, even if that means talking in the hammock while my mother-in-law takes our daughters for a walk in the woods nearby. On our most recent date we got some coconut milk steamed teas and went to a documentary screening about something we were both interested in. Sometimes our dates are at home after the kids go to bed. No matter what, we make time to do something together and talk. – Marcus

* **Laugh together**. Have inside jokes, go see a comedian, be silly together, share a funny video, do whatever it takes. Laughter helps you both reduce stress and feel closer to each other. Sometimes it helps remind you why you fell in love with your spouse in the first place because you like having fun together. Life has plenty of seriousness to it, so we have to carve out time to laugh with each other. Laughter is also a great help during times of hardship.

I just love to see Ashley smile when we are having a good time. It shows me she is happy with me and that we can both continue to enjoy being silly, sharing jokes, and laughing. Sometimes life gets serious and stressful, and we need to find the laughter in our everyday life. Finding the humor in challenges is part of what has helped us come through so much together without a lot of conflict. – Marcus

* Ask your spouse about their day. Ask your spouse what he or she is learning. What interests them lately? What they are reading? What is stressing them out? What do they want to accomplish? Bring yourself into their world, and allow them into yours as well. As you know, empathetic listening is one of the biggest components of communication in marriage. As humans, we all want to be heard and understood. Practice empathetic listening in your marriage.

Every day we text each other and check-in on how each other's day is going. I work outside the home while Ashley works in our home. Being able to check-in with each other with a simple, "How is your day going?" helps us to stay in sync and still support each other while we are apart. When I get home, we talk more in-depth about the events of the day. – Marcus

* Agree to disagree. Arguments that turn into emotionally charged fights could be detrimental to your intimacy as a married couple. Name calling or insults, cannot be taken back as easily as they are said. Think before you speak. Remember the golden rule, and treat your spouse how you want to be treated. Talk to your spouse the same way you want to be spoken to: with respect. Take a break to calm down if you need to. Before either you or your spouse escalates a disagreement, say something to calm the storm.

We are two very different and strong-willed people, so we obviously do not agree on everything. We can agree to disagree on the issues that do not need a solution right away or on problems that do not necessarily have a right or a wrong

answer. For issues that need a decision made, we can talk it out and listen to each other's point of view empathetically to come up with a solution. If I feel my patience wearing thin and my frustration or anger rising, I usually press pause on the conversation. I tell Marcus let's finish this discussion after I calm down. Mindless arguments are not worth the stress, and neither are emotional ones. – Ashley

* **Celebrate your successes together.** We thoroughly enjoy it when one of us reaches a personal goal and when we achieve our goals as a couple. When one of us is winning, we're both winning, because marriage is a team effort. Celebrate together, no matter how small of a success you achieve. Not every goal you reach needs a big party and fancy dinner. Plan what fits your family and budget.

When we hit one of our financial goals, we arranged to take the girls bowling and have a family date-night. It was fun to hit that goal and celebrate in some small way together. We used to get a bottle of sparkling cider and pour it into champagne glasses with dinner, toasting to whatever goal we had achieved. – Ashley

* **Learn how to communicate effectively.** Communication is vital to any relationship; in marriage, it is indispensable. Have a discussion about something you are both passionate about. Talk about your relationship and the overall state of your marriage. Where are you now and where do you want to be? For more on how to communicate with your spouse without fighting, check out our book *Communication in*

Marriage: How to Communicate with Your Spouse Without Fighting. In this book, we share how we went from not being able to communicate with each other, to communicating effectively without fighting.

* Create a bedtime routine. Routines will help you feel connected and create a safety net between the two of you. Create a night-time routine with some simple acts you can do together to help you connect before bed. Take a bath together, have a glass of tea, or talk for an hour while you hold hands and snuggle. Other bedtime routines you can do are going to bed at the same time, or saying goodnight and kissing each other before going to bed. Find something that fits the two of you, and start it today.

* Have each other's back. Support your spouse in any way you can. Help your spouse feel confident in their belief that they can achieve their goals, and that even if they fail, it will be okay. Be each other's comfort when one of you fails at something, because failure is a learning experience.

Empower your spouse to fight their own battles. Be there for your spouse in whatever way they need you. You want to create a safe environment for your marriage. In other words, your marriage should be a safe haven where both of you can be vulnerable with each other and you both feel safe enough to do so.

In our experience, there will be many moments when you have to have each other's back. For example, we had to deal with setting and enforcing boundaries. When we didn't want our girls to be forced into physical affection with anyone, including family members, we had to display a united front and verbalize to our family that we were promoting bodily autonomy. We wanted our girls to know they were not to be pressured into any physical interaction that they were uncomfortable with. We had nothing personal against any of our family members, but this was our boundary, and they needed to respect it.

Another hurdle for us was that a lot of the ways we decided to parent were very different than most of my family's. I breastfed each of our girls well past the age of twelve months, and decided to let them self-wean when they were ready. This was very shocking and even distasteful to many family members. Marcus having my back, knowing I had his full support, and even him having to step in and verbalize this support when certain family members would say something, meant so much to me. – Ashley

One way I felt supported by Ashley was when I lost my job while pursuing my college degree and we had our first daughter. I was laid off right before Christmas. Things were tight before the loss, but even moreso after. We had saved as much as we could for this kind of emergency, but that can only last so long. I felt overwhelmed and unsure. I had no way of knowing what was going to happen or how we could put food on the table or fuel in the tank. I was concerned, to say the least. As a man, not being able to provide for my family made me feel like I was a failure. I felt supported by Ashley because she made it clear to me she understood my frustrations and stress. She assured me I was not a failure and that we would get through this difficult time and be able to look back on this someday and appreciate what we overcame together. – Marcus

* **Give them the benefit of the doubt.** If your spouse forgets to do something you asked, give them the benefit of the doubt. Even better, do it for them. Little things that they forgot to do, like taking out the garbage or remembering to start the dishwasher, can go a long way in helping you both appreciate each other and keep resentment from growing.

Whenever I get frustrated that Marcus forgot to do something I asked, I try to take a step back and see exactly what he has going on. It is usually because he was busy doing other things for me, or for the business, that needed to be done and he ran out of time before he left for work. Sometimes he just forgets, and I cut him some slack because I forget things all the time too. – Ashley

* **Teamwork.** Budget together. Clean together. Cook together. Do the chores together. Split up the household to-do list or work on the list together, side-by-side. Things get done quicker, and it's nice having your spouse's company. Blast some music and have fun while you're at it.

* **Date night.** Take time for just the two of you to see each other as a couple, not just as parents, but also as two people who fell in love. Whether you take a walk around the block holding hands and talking, whether you stay in or go out, make this time focused on you as a couple a priority. Depending on

your financial situation, you can hire a sitter or ask friends, family or in-laws to help take care of your kids while you spend quality time together.

* **Say I love you.** Think about what your spouse brings to your life. Do they know how much they mean to you and how much they contribute to your happiness? Let your actions and words show your spouse without a shadow of a doubt that you love them, that you respect and value their opinion. Let your spouse know that you appreciate what they contribute to your life and that you see your spouse as an equal.

We all show our gratitude in different ways. I feel most appreciated by Ashley when she tells me how much she values everything I do. Sometimes I get a text from her saying, "Thank you for emptying the dishwasher." Or she tells me how much she appreciates the fact that I got up early with our toddlers and let her sleep in on my day to sleep in. When she verbalizes her gratitude and her love for me, I receive it best. When she does acts of service, I also feel loved by her. She makes my snacks for work, turkey salad for my lunches, and puts in a lot of effort to make my life a little easier. – Marcus

I really feel loved and appreciated when Marcus tells me how much he values everything I do. He thanks me and does things to help out around the house, or plays with our girls while I get some time to myself. Recently, he told me how much he truly values my input on his projects, and that made me feel loved and appreciated by him. – Ashley

When you are facing hard decisions, ask your spouse to weigh in on the issue. Hear their opinions on the things you do and take them to heart. Take their opinions seriously because they want to contribute to this relationship and your success, too. Furthermore, it brings them into your world, the world you create together, and it strengthens intimacy. Don't be afraid to brag about your spouse to your spouse. Be proactive in speaking positively about your spouse to everyone. This promotes an affirmative and unmitigated relationship of trust and admiration in your marriage, which enhances intimacy.

* **Write one reason you are thankful for your spouse everyday for 30 days.** It should be something different every single day. When you are done, give it to your spouse to read. Talk with your spouse about each of those thirty things you were thankful for on each particular day. You can even do this challenge together.

* **Show how you care about your kids**. If you are parents, showing your love for your children can go a long way toward strengthening that bond between you and the family you have created by getting married.

It always makes me feel loved when Marcus lets me know he appreciates me as a mother just as much, if not more, than being a wife. Motherhood is such a huge part of who I am, and to be recognized for my efforts in being the best mother I can be is encouraging. This makes me feel connected to Marcus because I feel he appreciates me, he sees my efforts, and he loves this big part of my identity.

When I see Marcus playing with our girls, coloring, letting them paint his toenails, dressing up and dancing ballet, my heart definitely swoons. – Ashley

Seeing Ashley playing with our kids and enjoying her role as a mother makes me appreciate her and love her more. It makes me proud to know I made the right choice in choosing her as a wife and mother to our children. I really enjoy going out and having picnics with our girls as a family, and thinking back to when it was just the two of us all those years ago.

When Ashley tells me that she thinks I am a great father to our girls, I feel fulfilled. I feel successful and that I am making continual progress because no one is perfect. On some days, I am a great dad; other days I feel I could do better. When she acknowledges my efforts, it really makes me feel euphoric and emotionally connected to her. – Marcus

Parenthood is not all we are; we are wives, husbands, and individuals. Being seen in each role helps us to be connected and develop that deep intimacy, because, after all, intimacy is "into-me-see". Being able to connect each part of ourselves and have the freedom to express our individuality with each other solidifies that connection and promotes intimacy.

Relationships are so important for the health of any person. You know the saying, "You are the average of the five people you surround yourself with." It is true. Focus on the people and relationships with which you surround yourself and your marriage. Are these relationships encouraging you to have a healthy and fulfilling marriage and life? Are these relationships holding you to a better standard or pulling you down? Re-evaluate the different relationships you have around you, and see if there are any changes you need to make.

WAYS THAT WE CONNECT AS A COUPLE WITH OUR CHILDREN

» Sliding in the snow.

» Camping without distractions, even if it is just in our living room.

» Bowling.

» Reading together before bed each night.

» Family game nights.

» Saying yes to something we normally say no to.

» Drawing something or coloring together.

» Building something with them – a snowman or Legos are always fun.

» Spending a day at a museum or aquarium together.

» Learning yoga together.

» Asking them about their favorite things.

» Giving them a compliment about something they struggle with or have been working on.

» Looking through recipe books, and letting them pick out a dinner to make with us. We even take them shopping to get the items needed. Homemade pizza is always a fun project.

» Telling them we believe in them.

» Hiking together. Getting out into the fresh air and packing a picnic lunch.

» Taking them to a concert, ballet, or to see one of their favorite characters live.

» Being silly and laughing together.

» Making cards for friends and relatives, or putting up decorations together for whatever holiday is coming up next.

» Having a tea party (real or pretend).

» Crafting something together. Pinterest is full of ideas.

» Going for a bike ride together. We like to ride to a local store and get kombucha and fruit as a treat.

» Telling them how happy we are to be their parents, and how proud of them we are.

» Going to a pick-your-own farm and getting some fresh fruit like apples, strawberries, blueberries, plums, oranges, raspberries, or whatever. Then taking some of that fruit to make smoothies, fruit salad, applesauce, fruit leather or preserves together.

» Making or buying a bird feeder, then watch for what birds come and identify them together.

» Go out on a one-on-one date with each child.

» Just listening to them, giving them our undivided attention and showing interest in what they have to say is one of the best ways to connect with our children.

» Asking them the best part of their day as well as the most challenging part.

» Having everyone go around the table at dinner every week and tell each other one thing we appreciate about them.

OTHER FUN WAYS TO CONNECT AS A COUPLE WITH YOUR CHILDREN

» Skiing. (Cross country, downhill, or water.)

» Rock climbing.

» Horseback riding.

» Miniature golfing.

» Sit around a campfire and have conversations.

» Go karting.

» Fishing.

» Tubing or other water sports.

» Write a story together. It can be fun for you to each start a story, switch papers and continue each other's story. Then continue swapping back and forth until you think it's finished. Read your story aloud, and see how funny your stories sound.

» Go to a yard sale and find something to fix up together.

» Help them learn to roller skate, ice skate or roller blade.

» Listen to an audio book or podcast together.

QUESTIONS TO ASK YOURSELF AND YOUR SPOUSE

» Ask your spouse daily, "What can I do for you today?"

» How do you feel the closest connection with each other in all your different roles: individuals, husband/wife, parents, etc.

» What is one way you can improve your relational connection this week?

» What do you appreciate about your spouse today?

GET TO KNOW YOUR SPOUSE AND YOURSELF

How do you feel connected relationally? Write down 5 ways with specific examples, so your spouse knows how best to connect with you. Then make it a point to do at least one thing your spouse listed every day.

Spouse A

1.

2.

3.

4.

5.

Spouse B

1.

2.

3.

4.

5.

Chapter 5
SOCIAL CONNECTION

"Only through our connectedness to others can we really
know and enhance the self. And only through working on
the self can we begin to enhance our connectedness to others."

– Harriet Goldhor Lerner

Social connection is a primal need for us as humans. There are various studies coming to light about the loss, or lack, of connection being the root of addiction and other behavioral problems. Social connection is a huge part of marriage because you are choosing to live a life with a companion and create your own community together as a unit.

Social connection with your spouse can happen in different ways: living together every day, going out on dates, going to parties and activities, family gatherings, basically doing life! Social connection touches almost every part of your marriage. Making sure this social bond is solidified, and the most enjoyable experience possible is in both of your hands. Taking time out for just the two of you to do an activity together is integral to developing a deeper intimacy. Make sure to take the time to include more social meet-ups as well with a group of friends you both enjoy, going to family gatherings together, and the like.

Social connection does more for your marriage than meets the eye. Feeling that connectivity can lead to health benefits or help you break bad habits. According to Dr. Emma M. Sepal, "Social connection strengthens our immune system ...helps us recover from disease faster, and may even lengthen our life. People who feel more connected to others have lower rates of anxiety and depression. Moreover, studies show they also have higher self-esteem, are more empathic to others, more trusting and cooperative and, as a consequence, others are more open to trusting and cooperating with them" (www. psychologytoday.com). Who doesn't want to add a few years onto their life? Who wouldn't want a boost to their immune system and a healthy body?

Social connection within your marriage is integral because your spouse is the person you spend most of your time and energy with. Your spouse is the person that has the most influence on your life. Focusing on making the connection you share together a positive one can aid you in reaping the benefits mentioned.

How can you start creating this positive environment in your relationship, or keep it going? Through connecting intentionally. Life gets busy; distractions come and go, other times life can get too routine. One good way to stay on the same page is to cultivate a social calendar that works for each of you. You don't want to get too busy and not take the time to enjoy the moment together. We feel too much busyness goes against our goal of having a peaceful family, so we intentionally plan our calendar every month. We make sure to keep two weekends a month with nothing going on. During these times, we stay home, we take our girls to parks, on bike rides, on hikes, to museums, and other family bonding or learning experiences. Life is about experiences, after all! For weekends that we have events, we try to plan our Sundays to be empty for whatever we feel like doing, just the four of us; and occasionally, just the two of us.

Put in the effort to carve out time for just the two of you to get out and do something together. See a concert, a movie, hike, play a sport or game, have a meal, get a coffee and talk or whatever you enjoy doing to reconnect while getting out of the house. Schedule your time to connect, because when life gets busy, it is too easy to forget and put time together on the shelf. By scheduling time together, your connection remains a priority.

One of our favorite things to do is to find a teahouse. Neither of us are big coffee drinkers, so finding a unique teahouse and enjoying the fancy teapots and specialized flavors, while getting to snuggle up together and talk about life, is pretty special for us. – Ashley

If you cannot get out of the house because of your children's needs, then turn your kitchen table into a Ping-Pong match after they go to bed. Set up a fancy dinner with candles and special dishes while your little ones watch a movie. Play a board game, word game, or cards. Sit together and enjoy a hot cup of tea or hot chocolate and reminisce about your past or dream about your future. Find something you can do together. Go out with friends, both solo and as a couple. Respect each other while you are away as well as when you are together, always speaking positively of your spouse. If you disrespect your spouse, whether you are alone with your friends or with your spouse in a group, you can damage the bond you have been working on, your trust, and the connection between both of you. Your spouse should be the safest place to turn to, and you, in turn, should be a safe haven for them.

Getting out and doing things with other people is important, but not always feasible for all couples. Invite friends over; find other couples with children to enjoy each other's company. Find ways that work for you both to be social.

For the first four and a half years of our marriage, we lived in rural Vermont. Okay, most of Vermont is rural, but this was a dirt road with a handful of neighbors on it. The closest city for grocery shopping, besides small general stores and gas stations, was a forty-five-minute drive. I think we had one blinking light in the town, not even a stoplight.

There were not many people our age around, and no one really that we were able to connect with on a friendship level. Our closest friends lived, again, forty-five minutes away. Besides the occasional meet up with those friends, all we had were family gatherings. That was okay for that season of our life. Now we are living near the city and have many more friends, and we are invited to many more social events. Now we have to say no sometimes, and balance our calendar (and budget!) so we don't get too busy. – Ashley

Whether you are an introvert or extrovert, social connection can benefit you, your spouse, and your marriage. Ashley has made more relationships with other moms and sets up play dates and activities throughout the week for her and the girls. Marcus enjoys being social once in a while with other people. He is more of an introvert, and finds it harder to meet friends that have similar interests. That's okay. We find out what works for our personalities and marriage, and strike a balance; you should do the same. What works for our marriage, might not work for yours. You can develop your own unique way that is successful for the social connection you both crave.

Family gatherings can be a great way to connect with your extended family as a couple. Some couples make a weekly dinner appointment with their in-laws, while others do it much more infrequently. Balance is the key to social activities in your marriage. We have said it a million times, but harmony in all parts of your life is essential for a happy, connected couple.

I enjoy going to family events with Ashley's family because I get to learn more about them and how unique everyone is. The different conversations are a nice way to see the various perspectives and learn to see things through her relatives' worldview. It is nice to catch up with the extended family every once in a while. For the most part, we see our in-laws and Ashley's grandparents and enjoy a big dinner together. I love having the big meal with the variety of foods that we all bring together. – Marcus

I have never met Marcus's mother in person, my mother-in-law. She doesn't speak English very much, and I don't speak her language well enough to speak over the phone. We use Marcus to exchange our well wishes between each other. We see my mom and stepdad usually no less than once a month, sometimes twice. This works for us well. – Ashley

As in all areas of marriage, you must find your boundaries and comfort levels. Come up with a compromise that works for both of you to feel connected to each other, your extended family, and friends. Your marriage is always the priority, but those other relationships and social connections can enhance your marriage connection as long as they are healthy and positive.

Recently, I met a friend for tea at a coffee shop, and Marcus stayed home with our girls. I thought I would only be an hour, but it turned into three! It felt so good to be out alone having a conversation without all the little interruptions and distractions. I needed that. I needed to recharge my batteries, have some adult conversations that didn't have to be censored for little listening ears, and enjoy that independence. Of course, I was even happier to go home to my wonderful husband and amazing daughters. I needed that external social connection so I could be better at connecting with my husband and children. It gave me the much-needed break I required to fill my cup, so I had more to give to my family. – Ashley

Being out with friends gives us the opportunity to talk about ourselves and hear our friends talk about what is most important to them. Usually, your spouse or significant other will come up in conversation. These situations can be a great reminder of how much you really appreciate your spouse, their partnership, and how much they actually do for you.

When I get to play pick up soccer and have that time to myself, or to talk at length with one of my friends on the phone uninterrupted, I feel recharged. I feel like I am not missing out on the things, or people, that were a big part of my life before I met my wife or before I became a father. – Marcus

Connecting with your spouse through different social situations can happen in many ways. Sometimes, going out to a social event or coffee shop meeting on your own and coming back refreshed to your spouse enhances that connection. Other times, that connection is solidified when you see your spouse make an effort to spend time with your family, or encourages you to have a girls'/guys' night. Supporting your spouse in all areas of your marriage, being willing to compromise and listening to what your spouse needs will strengthen your bond and intimacy.

SIMPLE WAYS TO CONNECT SOCIALLY
WITH YOUR SPOUSE

* **Create new traditions**. When you come together and create a new family with your spouse, you bring together different family traditions that you can choose to keep going,

alter or discontinue. You can find new traditions to start that are important to you both. This brings you closer because you are molding the customs in your life to fit your relationship. Carrying on the traditions in your marriage together brings you closer because you are both counting on these events and looking forward to experiencing them together.

* **Cheer your spouse on in competition, races or join in with them.** Supporting your spouse in what he is interested in is one way of enhancing the intimacy between you both. Entering a color run can be a creative way to connect or a 5K race to benefit a charity, support a good cause, and get some exercise. Obstacle courses are gaining popularity and would be a great team building challenge for the both of you if you enjoy physical activity. Paint and sip nights at your local art gallery are great for any couple looking to enjoy some wine and creative time together.

I love anything crafty. I was making silver-wire and semi-precious stone jewelry for a while, and it was helping to pay the bills. I signed up for a bazaar, and Marcus came with me to keep me company while I sold my wares. It was really nice to have him with me to help and just to spend that time together doing something I really loved. It was definitely a way to help us connect. – Ashley

I really enjoyed Ashley sitting in the bleachers watching me play pick-up soccer. I was having a great time playing my favorite sport and knowing she was there to support me. – Marcus

* **Experience something new together.** Learn a new sport or activity together. Travel to new places or explore a new city or country together. We learned tennis one summer together and had a blast. It is also fun to plan a weekend getaway. Try a new restaurant that neither of you have been to or plan a vacation to a different destination.

* **Pick fruit together.** Get out with a group of friends, family, or just the two of you and support your local farmers. Depending on where you live and what you can pick, this event can become a fun tradition for you both. Every year, we pick strawberries, blueberries, apples, pumpkins, or cherries. Every fall, we look forward to picking the apples and pumpkins while drinking hot apple cider and enjoying homemade donuts.

* **Reconnect with your interests and passions.** Continue finding time to enjoy the things you love to do so that you do not lose your identity. Your spouse fell in love and chose to be with you because of who you are. Your interests are a big part of your identity. Your interests will change and evolve throughout your life, but it is important to keep doing those healthy and positive hobbies that give you enjoyment in addition to being a spouse, parent, and friend. You will be a better spouse because of it.

* **Be happy.** Are you happy with yourself and life? If you are not happy with your life, how can you have a happy marriage? How can you connect or reconnect with your spouse? Finding your identity, cultivating your own social, personal acceptance

and outlets will aid you in creating the intimate closeness you desire with your spouse. Your happiness is in your hands. If you waste time waiting for, " If I only had X," or, "If I was thinner I would be happy, if I achieved X I would be happy," your life will pass you by.

QUESTIONS TO ASK YOURSELF AND YOUR SPOUSE

» What are some ways you feel socially content and connected with your spouse?

» What is one thing you can work on this week to enhance that connection?

» Do you feel like you are getting enough social connection with your friends and family?

GET TO KNOW YOUR SPOUSE AND YOURSELF

How do you feel connected socially? Write down 5 ways with specific examples, so your spouse knows how to best connect with you. Then make it a point to do at least one thing your spouse listed every day.

Spouse A

1.

2.

3.

4.

5.

Spouse B

1.

2.

3.

4.

5.

Chapter 6
Physical & Sexual Intimacy

"Intimacy is not purely physical. It's the act of connecting with someone so deeply, you feel like you can see into their soul."

– Unknown

Physical touch with your spouse will keep that spark ignited, grow your friendship, and help you feel connected. Holding hands when you drive in the car, sitting next to each other at the table, and snuggling up together on the couch, are all ways you can remain close. Hugging goodbye each morning after a passionate kiss to let your spouse know you enjoyed last night. Giving your spouse's butt a squeeze to let her know you think she's sexy. Wrapping your arms around your spouse while he does the dishes and kissing his neck or cheek lets him know you appreciate and love him. These are all ways you can use touch to enhance physical connection with your spouse.

Touch is used for pleasure, comfort, safety, assurance, encouragement, and so much more. Making sure you keep a steady flow of physical contact with your spouse can do great things for intimacy in your marriage. For some people, passionate physical touch or physical intimacy is how they feel and express love, comfort, and security. Physical touch is one of the *5 love languages.* Find out the love language that you and your spouse each speak by taking the free online quiz at www.5lovelanguages.com.

When Marcus maintains physical contact with me throughout the day through hand holding, wrapping his arms around me, and just sitting close to me, I feel connected to him. I feel satisfied in that connection, and I usually want more of a sexual connection. – Ashley

Author Paulo Coelho said, "Anyone who is in love is making love the whole time, even when they're not. When two bodies meet, it is just the cup overflowing. They can stay together for hours, even days. They begin the dance one day and finish it the next, or–such is the pleasure they experience–they may never finish it." You know the saying that sex starts in the kitchen. It means sexual intercourse is the climax of your physical intimacy, but it's not the beginning. Physical intimacy starts from the moment you wake up and roll over to give you spouse a kiss on the forehead, or wake up snuggled in each other's arms. It continues throughout your day as you make each other breakfast, kiss goodbye or hug hello, hold hands on the way to work, and spend time in the evening together talking about your day while sitting close.

When you have kids who are toddlers or babies, it can be very difficult to find time to connect and have deep conversations. The best thing to do is to catch the few minutes of time when your little ones do not need your attention, and do small things, like passionate kisses and hugs. When you make good use of these small pockets of uninterrupted time, you will be able to maintain the physical connection you have together. Even though they aren't physical, acts of service also contribute to your physical intimacy. When Ashley makes graham crackers for Marcus to take to work, or when Marcus remembers to leave the onions out of the stir-fry for Ashley, we are serving each other out of love and respect. In turn, we want to express our love to one another physically. All of these things contribute to your physical intimacy with your spouse.

Just recently, we had a misunderstanding about physical touch. Ashley had expressed to me that she didn't feel pursued by me. She wanted me to touch her more throughout the day, message her a text with more than, "How is your day going?" I was really busy at work the day after, and I didn't message her until shortly before I came home, and it was just talking about dinner and our day. I also compartmentalize things, so when I am at work, that is all I think about.

Despite what the media in America would have you think, not all men have sex on their minds all the time. So when I got home, I made a point to hold Ashley and have some physical touch. She was not very receptive. That evening we went to bed, and I thought she was tired and laid down on my side. We had to have another conversation because I did not understand what exactly she needed from me.

Occasionally, we need to have more than one conversation if an issue isn't resolved. Sometimes, we have to ask exactly what our spouse means because we have two different under-standings. I know she is not a light switch (that's the analogy she used- a light switch that easily turns on) and really thought about what she was trying to express to me.

She needed more romancing, more connection throughout the day. Even if it was a text from work telling her how much I miss her, or how much I am looking forward to coming home to her. She wanted to feel wanted and desired by me, even if I didn't want to make love. It can be easy to let those little things that we took for granted in the beginning of our relationships fade away. To keep that fire ignited, we have to keep feeding it. I realized I had to be more intentional in this area for my wife and our marriage. – Marcus

Physical intimacy is not the only connection needed to sustain a healthy sex life. Sometimes we get that physical connection solely through sex, because we have been apart. Sex itself can be a great way to get that deeper connection with each other. Connecting in a way that you cannot be intimate with anyone else, barring your souls to each other, opening your bodies to one another is the most straightforward way of intimacy. This won't work all the time, though. Purely physical sex is shallower than a deeper emotionally intimate sexual experience. As we mentioned, emotional connection is integral to sexual intimacy. A strong emotional connection leads to satisfying and passionate sex.

Your sex life should be a mix of that raw physical sex and the emotionally intimate driven experience of making love.

Can it be both at the same time? Of course! The important thing is to remember to be intentional with your physical affection and keep sex a priority in your marriage. After having kids, physical intimacy gets more challenging. That doesn't mean you put your physical connection on the back burner, it just means you have to be more intentional about it and put in more of an effort.

Children bring many joys and a purpose to our lives, they also present more challenges. Being touched out after a long day of being with toddlers occurs frequently in our house. I let Marcus know when I need a break from being touched so he can help me get some alone time. I will take a shower or just go upstairs and lay down for thirty minutes (or for as long as he can keep them away!). – Ashley

Physical connection does not always have to be about sex. That is a complaint we hear quite often, actually. If you feel like the physical touch and connection is lacking in your relationship, aside from sex, the first thing is to verbalize it to your spouse. Sit down and ask each other the questions in this chapter. Implement these ideas one at a time until they become your reaction. Physical connection in marriage is just as important as sexual intimacy. We have said it a million times: your spouse is not a mind reader! You have to tell them. If they don't get it, try showing them. If they are truly resistant, there may be something deeper going on, and you both should consider counseling to help you get to the bottom of it. Let them know how important physical intimacy is to you. Any loving and equal partner will make an effort to help you feel loved and connected.

Make time to hold your spouse. One of the most amazing ways to feel close is to be naked and spooning, even if you are not going to have sex. Sleep naked! Cuddle for a minute when you wake up instead of hopping right out of bed. That skin-to-skin contact has many benefits to humans. The love hormone Oxytocin is released, a connection is made, and you get to just be together. Lie on your spouse's chest and listen to their heartbeat or give each other a massage.

Have you asked your spouse how and where they like to be touched? Do they like you to hold their hand when you are running errands or sitting together? Do they prefer you give them a long hug before leaving for work or a lingering kiss? Do they like their forehead kissed? Some people like to have their partner play with their hair, or brush their hair. Have you ever painted your spouse's nails or shaved their beard? These are acts of service that involve physical connection, and are simple ways you can display your affection physically. Find out what you each want and make it happen to bring that physical closeness as regularly as you can. *Touch your spouse without having an expectation of having sex.*

I really enjoy having Ashley shave my beard for me. When she shaves for me, it is a way I feel connected and appreciated. She is taking the time to take care of me, and it saves me from doing it. The physical closeness is very much appreciated, and it requires a level of trust with the sharp blades.

Hugs and sex help me feel physically connected to Ashley. She feels connected by the same things but also needs more. It is each of our duties to find out how each other feels that connection and make an effort to stay connected physically with our spouse. – Marcus

Sit and watch the fire, or stars together as you talk about your hopes and dreams, laughing together or just sitting quietly enjoying one another's company as you are cuddling close. Don't ever stop pursuing your spouse; there is always more to learn about them. Help them feel wanted and desired by asking them how they want you to show that physically and in all ways. For physical, non- sexual touches, try hugging and holding hands. If you are not used to being physically touched, it will be awkward at first but will become second nature after some time.

Sit facing each other with your legs and arms intertwined sitting or laying down. Stare into each other's eyes for three to five minutes. Set a timer and put all distractions away. This exercise can help you start to form physical intimacy while your bodies are connected, and your eyes are searching for that deeper communion with your spouse.

If your spouse won't take action, you may need to pioneer these early steps. For example, if your spouse will not give you random hugs and kisses, take the first step and hug them. While you hug him or her, say something in their ear that you appreciate about them. It could even be something they did for you, like cleaning the dishes, letting you sleep in, folding laundry, or taking the trash out, etc. One thing you could do to help you remember is to choose a time that is convenient for you, like first or last thing before leaving home, first thing after coming back home, or when you wake up in the morning.

Considering our skin is the largest organ of our bodies, we cannot neglect how essential physical touch is for you, your spouse, and your marriage. Physical touch is the first thing a new baby longs for as it enters this world. That physical connection calms the infant, regulates their stress hormones and even body temperature. So, ask your spouse this simple question today, "How do you want to be touched?"

OTHER WAYS TO CONNECT PHYSICALLY WITHOUT HAVING SEX

» Lie in bed and talk about life together.

» Go for a walk around your neighborhood hand-in-hand.

» Have a picnic together.

» Give each other a massage. Watch some videos, get some books from the library and learn how to hit all those pressure points so your spouse can thoroughly enjoy being rubbed down by you.

» Send a flirty text, or sext.

» If possible, sit down or lay down with your spouse when you get home from work and talk about your day.

» Cook dinner together with music.

» Dance around in your living room.

» Exercise together.

» Tell your spouse how much you appreciate them while keeping eye contact and are cuddling them.

» Make out. It doesn't need to lead to sex, but make sure you take the time to kiss passionately. Restore some of those butterfly feelings and enjoy the closeness.

» Hold hands. Try spicing it up by running your fingers over their hand, kissing their fingertips, and spelling out flirty words while you talk about your relationship.

» Take a nap together.

» Put your hands around their waist.

» Hug your spouse from behind.

» Shower or bathe together.

» Look at pictures together. Pictures from your wedding, when you were dating, trips you have taken or when you were children.

» Plan a fun date together.

» Cuddle for twenty minutes. Lie in your spouse's arms on the bed, or sit on the couch. No distractions, just being close to each other physically. Talk about your dreams or just enjoy the closeness in the silence.

» Be open and vulnerable with each other. You cannot be truly physically close if you don't open up to your spouse emotionally.

» Hug your spouse for an extended amount of time each day. Try a one-minute hug, and then extend it to however long you both want. That physical contact helps release that love hormone cocktail from your brain.

» Take care of your appearance. Dress up, put on that perfume you know your spouse likes, take a nice long hot shower, have a fresh shave, whatever you want.

» Create your own sexy game together.

» Go on a second honeymoon or recreate special parts of your original honeymoon.

» Dance to your wedding song together.

» Be more touchy-feely. Aim for lots of skin-to-skin contact because that is what makes your brain give you that rush of chemicals that trigger the happy, loving feelings. Sleeping together naked is a great way to enforce and take full advantage of your body's connection systems. You or your spouse might not be comfortable enough with a show of public display of affection. This is no excuse not to have physical contact with your spouse throughout the day, or hold hands when out and about.

» Compliment each other. Complimenting your spouse can go a lot further than you might realize when it is genuine.

SEXUAL INTIMACY

"Sex is always about emotions. Good sex is about free emotions; bad sex is about blocked emotions."

– Deepak Chopra

Sex is vital to a marriage. Sexual intimacy may be the most sacred part of your marriage. A sexless marriage is not a healthy marriage. There are so many more aspects to a sexual relationship in a marriage than just sexual intercourse. Sex is one way we get to know our spouse on a more physically intimate and sometimes spiritual level. Lack of sex in your marriage can make you feel unattractive, lonely, resentful, angry, frustrated, and unloved. The sad truth is this: being denied sex by your spouse is one of the loneliest feelings anyone can experience. However, the quality of your sexual intimacy is more important than quantity. In order to have satisfying sexual experiences with your spouse that lead to sexual intimacy, you have to be completely open and honest with each other.

That being said, we believe that complete honesty has been key to developing deep intimacy in not only our marriage but also in the successful marriages we know. Is there something you feel shy or embarrassed to talk to your spouse about? That may be a great place to start. To have true intimacy in a marriage, you must both be able to be completely naked with each other emotionally and intellectually as well as physically.

To have true intimacy is to completely know your spouse so you can connect with them to your fullest potential.

LET'S TALK SEX

Talking about sex with your spouse is a *must*. It may be uncomfortable at first, but the more you do it, the easier it will get. You need to be authentic with your spouse and devoted to openness about your sex life with your spouse. If you never ask, you won't receive. Have you and your spouse talked about what you like and don't like about in bed? If you want to have better sex, it starts by talking about sex with your spouse.

» What turns you on?

» What turns you off?

» Where are the spots that drive you crazy in a good way?

» Where are the places that drive you crazy in a bad way?

» What makes you uncomfortable?

» What are some things you want to try?

» What places do you want to have sex?

» What positions do you want to try?

» What toys do you want to experiment with?

» What types of sex do you want to try or absolutely are not comfortable with at this point?

» How often do you want to have sex each week?

» Who should initiate?

» Are you both satisfied with the amount of foreplay?

» Are you both happy with how often you have oral sex?

» Do you want your spouse to dominate in the bedroom?

» Do you like your hair pulled?

» Do you enjoy (or would you like) when your spouse grips your neck during sex? What intensity do you prefer? (Just a light grip, gently choking, or more aggressive?)

» Do you want to have sex when she has her period? What kinds of sex?

» Do you talk about her menstrual cycle and how the different hormone surges make sex feel during the different stages of her cycle?

» Do you each climax every time? How often? Can you climax multiple times?

» How does your spouse initiate sex? How do you?

» When does sex pop into your mind?

» Do you believe effective communication is integral to amazing sex?

» Is our sex life satisfying to you? Why or why not?

» What does satisfying sex mean to you?

» How do you feel when you want to make love with me, and I don't want to?

» Be honest, when does sex feel like a chore to you?

» Do you feel insecure with your body, especially when it comes to sex or being naked in front of me?

» When do you look forward to sex the most?

» When does sex feel more like work than fun?

» Have you ever used sex as leverage in our marriage? Why?

» What makes you feel overwhelmed?

» If I let you dress me for a wild night of passionate and unforgettable sex, what clothes would you put on me? (If any)

» What is the sexiest thing I do in bed that you love the most?

» Have you ever been sexually abused in any way?

» What is something different you want to do in the bedroom?

» Have you ever lied (or not told the complete truth) about how much you enjoyed my performance just so I did not feel hurt? (i.e. faking it)

» What am I not doing for you to make our sex life amazing, in and out of our bedroom?

» What don't you like about our sex life or something I do during sex?

» Are you unsatisfied with our sex life in any way? If yes, why?

» How can I show you that I am sexually attracted to you?

» Do you struggle with sexual temptation?

» What do you need to be in the mood for sex?

» Do you feel uncomfortable initiating sex?

» How do you feel after we have sex?

» What makes you feel uncomfortable about sex?

» What do you want to do after we are done having sex?

» Do you feel safe with me?

No questions are off limits when you talk about sex with your spouse. You should both be ready to be open-minded and listen to what your spouse needs, and see how you can find a compromise you both can enjoy. Your sex life will evolve over the course of your marriage, but you should always be connecting sexually. The things that you like today may not turn you on tomorrow. It could work one day and not the next. That's why an open dialog about your sexual intimacy is imperative. Know instead of guessing because your spouse is not a mind reader.

We talked about how often we want to have sex a week as a minimum, and you should too. We had different numbers and compromised until we agreed. Sometimes we have more, but almost never less. Have you had that conversation? It is a question that you should ask each other more than once in your marriage. As with all things in life, you go through different seasons. Sometimes your sex drive will be higher, and sometimes it will be lower due to hormones, life situations, and changes. The important thing is to know what your spouse needs and let them know what you need. Keep an open dialog. If your spouse absolutely does not want to have sex when you want to, find out why. Do they not feel emotionally connected to you? If not, then what is needed to restore the connection?

Sometimes all you will have time for is a quickie. A straight to the point, I want you now, kind of sexual experience. When you are not in that moment, or maybe just not in the mood, make sure to take your time and use your hands all over each other's bodies. Lots and lots of foreplay. Let your sexual experience be intimate and slow sometimes. Mix it up. Try different positions, have soft, slow sex; fast, rough sex; slow, rough sex; whatever you both enjoy.

There are three different types of sex. First, the purely physical sex that holds its energy in the genital area – like quickies! Second, the emotional connection sex, where the energy is in your heart area. Lastly, there is the spiritual connective sex energy, which is hosted in your head. Sex has a bad reputation from the generations before us and because of the sex-saturated culture portrayed in the media. What if sex is meant to connect our spirits, renew life, and unite intimately with our spouse? What if sex was created to bring us closer to a heavenly ecstasy like an out of body experience? In the references section, there are some resources on this subject if you wish to delve a bit deeper.

You should absolutely never withhold sex from your spouse to punish them or to manipulate them into getting your way. (Not wanting to have sex because you are not in the mood is completely different.) Using your sacred sexual intimacy as a bargaining chip is not healthy for your marriage. Another reason for having a low sex drive could be an imbalance of hormones. If one of you feels that your sex drive is lower than it should be, or if sex is uncomfortable or painful, than make an appointment with your doctor to have your sex hormones checked, as well as a full thyroid panel done. Both men and women can have sex hormone imbalances.

Birth control can affect a woman's sex drive. Likewise, pregnancy increases sexual desires for some women and decreases for others. After a baby, postpartum hormones are usually all over the place. Menopause can cause many women to have a lower sex drive. Different times in a woman's menstrual cycle can cause her sex drive to increase or decrease. Usually during ovulation, her drive will be higher, and right after her period, she may have a lower sex drive. After her menstrual cycle is over, she may even be dryer and need the help of some coconut oil or other lubricant.

When Ashley was pregnant with our first child, I was sometimes scared to have sex with her. I thought she or our baby would get hurt, and it would be painful for her. I did some research and felt better after talking to Ashley and she assured me that the baby would not be hurt. I had the same feelings after she had our baby too because she had needed surgery. – Marcus

It will take time to become fully, sexually intimate like you were pre-pregnancy. Tiredness from work, sleepless nights with baby, caring for children will all take a physical toll on your body's ability and energy level for sex. Sex might not be enjoyable initially after the birth of your baby either. There are so many changes that happen throughout the pregnancy and birth process with hormones skyrocketing and then plummeting. Breastfeeding can also make a woman's sex drive plummet. It is all hormone related.

The one thing I did when I felt no sex drive was to look forward to the connection of sex, even though I didn't always have the drive. I found the more we had sex, the more my drive increased, depending on what part of the month since it depended on my hormone levels. We scheduled sex, and it was much needed at that time in our lives. I have now been breastfeeding for four years, and my sex drive is now higher. – Ashley

Give yourself a break, relax and know that this is just another season in your life. Your body and sex life will not always be this challenging. It will get better, and the best way to encourage growth is practice. Schedule sex, use lubricant, loosen up with some wine, take some time to yourself, and see a doctor if you feel it is necessary to calm your fears.

A good way to encourage your spouse after pregnancy would be to help with the house and the baby. Take some stress off of the main caregiver and run the bath. I know you may be tired after a long day at work, but so is she. Get things done as a team and you can have time to enjoy deep conversations, sex, or just relaxing on the couch. Make sure to show lots of physical affection.

Painful sex is, unfortunately, a reality for many people. Make sure to see a doctor and get all your sex hormones, including DHEA (which can act like testosterone in the body) checked. It may be a reaction to lubricant (try coconut oil!) or condoms. Or, it may be a complication from being circumcised. Our best advice would be to talk to a functional doctor who could point you in the right direction. Your low sex drive could also be because you are too tired. Are you too busy? Is there too much stress in your life? What can you cut out of your life? Is it the lack of connection in other areas of your marriage that leaves you uninterested in sex?

For some people, sexual intimacy is the way they feel emotionally connected. Without sex, they may not feel as close to their spouse emotionally. Research shows people who have been sexually abused may feel emotionally intimate through sex more than others. This also presents many other challenges. That is why complete vulnerability with each other, protection of your sexual experiences together, and open dialogue is so integral to your sexual intimacy.

If you are dealing with sexual challenges related or unrelated to sexual abuse or trauma, depression, low self-esteem or body image, we recommend you seek the help of a sex therapist or psychologist, both individually and together, sooner rather than later. Counseling can help guide you as you work through these challenges and offer great tools.

To have great sex, your body needs good blood flow. The flow of your blood will ensure every part of your body is receiving the nutrients it needs to function well and stimulate your sex organs. To have good blood flow, avoid the things that decrease it, such as sugar, drugs, or anything that makes you less healthy. Eat plenty of vegetables and fruits. Exercise and drink plenty of water. We are not health professionals, so please consult with your doctor before making any changes to your health routine.

Another very common issue related to sex is premature ejaculation. An overall healthy diet, specifically low in sugar, can help many men who struggle with this issue. Focusing on pleasuring your spouse before you ejaculate can help. Using the stop-start method has been proven to help many couples too. At the end of the day, if you both focus on pleasuring each other and have a lot of foreplay, it can go a long way towards make sex amazing for you both.

Your sexual experience is not only dependent on physical contributors, but also your emotional connection. How connected do you feel with your spouse emotionally? Are there any issues that need some attention in your marriage? Problem solving and releasing resentments can enormously improve your sex life. This all ties back to that open dialogue we keep mentioning. Complete honesty in your marriage is a must. We promise you, your sex life will benefit from your transparency inside and outside of the bedroom.

That being said, when you stop having sex with your spouse, you begin to feel like your spouse is just a roommate. Anger, resentment, and other issues will begin to have a negative impact on your marriage. The lack of sexual intimacy will open up your marriage to possibilities of infidelity, loneliness, feeling undesired, frustrations, anger, and could even end with divorce. You don't have to have sex every day to feel connected to your spouse. However, it should be frequent enough that you are both satisfied and happy with your sex life.

If you find it difficult to get back in bed with your spouse, try cuddling naked and discussing several of the sex questions in this book. Try not to overly criticize, and instead, let your spouse know what you enjoy in bed. Give each other a long kiss or hug, talk about the most amazing sex you have had as a couple. Talking about sex openly with your spouse is a sure way to deepen intimacy and connect with each other. On many occasions, it will prepare your mind and body for amazing sex. It is another example of foreplay to add to your sex life. Remember, sex starts in the mind.

What's more, a simple way to rekindle romance and your sex life is by following the three steps below:

First, build a safe haven in your home by treating each other with respect and kindness. Understand and do your best to meet your spouse's needs and earn each other's trust.

Second, display physical affection by touching and romancing each other physically throughout the day. Show your spouse how much you cherish him or her, and are attracted to every part of them.

Finally, have intellectual conversations to build your emotional connection by spending time together each day.

Doing these three simple, yet effective steps above will build up your intimacy and get your foreplay started, which will eventually help you to have the satisfying and passionate sex you both desire.

Mae West famously said, "Sex is an emotion in motion." Sex is the most tangible way we get to connect with our spouse. Intimacy in your sexual relationship will need honesty, safety, and emotional connection the most. Your spouse wants to feel loved and desired by you, and you by them. Sex is one of the most straightforward ways to fulfill this desire. Of course, your spouse wants to feel like more than just a sex object. Connecting in all areas of marriage and building that intimacy outside the bedroom will bring your sexual intimacy to places you never thought possible.

WAYS TO CONNECT SEXUALLY

* **Schedule sex.** Get it on the calendar. Have the talk, and figure out how many times you are going to engage in sexual activity together each week, and make it happen!

* **Pillow talk.** Stay in bed after you make love, and talk while you are lying next to each other.

* **Play games in the bedroom.** For some fun in the bedroom, you can play truth or dare, strip poker, strip checkers, basically anything that gets you both in the mood and naked.

* **Naked twister!** Have a drink and start spinning while your naked bodies get tangled. You may find some fun new positions to try out as well!

* Have sex in another room. Or any fun place you choose. Mixing up the places adds variety to your sexual experience together.

* **Lots of foreplay.** See how long you can truly pleasure each other before you just have to have each other. For a lot of women, foreplay is paramount to their overall sexual experience. Take. Your. Time.

* **Add some toys or props to your sexy time.** Handcuffs anyone? Blindfolds? C-rings? Sex pillows? Whatever works for both of you.

* Dirty talk. Need I say more? If you need ideas, try talking about what you are going to do to your spouse before, or while you are doing it.

* **Quickie.** Sometimes there is nothing hotter than the, "I want you right now, take your clothes off!" quickie.

* **Mix it up.** Slow, soft and sensual...fast, rough...slow, rough...you get the idea. Try something new!

* **Try at least three different positions.** More if you are feeling it.

* **Talk during sex.** Let your spouse know when they are hitting the spot, when something feels good. If it doesn't, or they are missing it, show them.

* Try something new. Try a fantasy one of you has shared. Is there something you have always wondered about? Now is your time to experiment. Of course, with some new things, it is important to discuss prior to sex to make sure your spouse is on board.

* **Start, stop.** Start sex at the beginning of the day, but don't finish. This may keep you rearing to go later on that day by prolonging your sexual pleasure and desire. It is like quickies until the real showdown later that day or night. If you can orgasm more than once, have fun!

* **Oral sex.** Take time to learn from your spouse what works for them. Do not make the mistake of reading from blogs or magazines what works. Every body is unique, and what works for your spouse will change over time, even on the day.

* **Be vocal.** Obviously, this is hard when you have children in the house, so take full advantage when it is possible. Sound machines or having a radio on can help mute some of the noises.

* **Surprise each other.** Let's say a wife schedules a night at a hotel and arrives there before her spouse. When they arrive, she's wearing nothing but sexy lingerie. Do something your spouse will never expect!

* **Role play/ made up scenarios for those looking for something even more risqué.** The possibilities are endless. Just remember to discuss this prior with your spouse so that no one feels uncomfortable.

* **Make love often.** At the *very least,* we recommend weekly. A healthy marriage has a healthy sex life. Keeping that sexual energy alive and well is so vital for your marriage and health too. Answer the questions about how often you each want to make love and commit to that minimum every week. Remember, a sexless marriage doesn't just happen overnight.

Lack of sexual intimacy is proven to cause resentment, create distance, and contribute to infidelity. You and your spouse can easily become roommates if your sex life is non-existent.

* **Make sure you are emotionally and mentally present during sex**. If you are not focused on your spouse and consummating your physical love and desire for each other, ask yourself why. Are you pre-occupied with something else? What can you do to better prepare yourself to be fully present? What can you do to prevent this from happening?

* **Don't just go for the big O.** Orgasm should not be the sole focus of making love to your spouse. Instead think of it as the perfect ending, the cherry on top of the sundae. Some women are able to orgasm multiple times, whereas men usually reach that crescendo and then need to rest and recharge. Foreplay, switching positions, and mixing it up can help lengthen your sexual pleasure and experience. Enjoy each other's bodies instead of stressing about orgasm.

* **Have a drink!** Having a glass or two of wine will help you relax and drop some of those inhibitions that may be holding you back in bed. This is especially helpful after you have been cleared for postpartum sex, or when one of you is more stressed or tense.

* **Prepare for sex throughout the day.** This is why scheduling, or just letting your partner know in advance that you want to make love that day, is helpful. You can spend the day listening to music that gets you in the mood or thinking about your sexy spouse- how much you love him, why you

appreciate her, how far you have come together because of their influence in your life.

* **Get a room.** Go to a bed and breakfast for the night, or the whole weekend.

* **Reminisce.** Spend some time remembering your first sexual encounter together and some of the amazing nights you've spent with your bodies intertwined.

QUESTIONS TO ASK YOURSELF AND YOUR SPOUSE

» How do you feel the most connected physically to your spouse?

» What is one way you can make an effort this week to enhance that physical connection between the two of you?

» What are three physical shows of affection you really enjoy from your spouse and you wish they would do more often?

» Are you or your spouse uncomfortable with physical or sexual intimacy? What is the root cause behind this?

» How do you feel the most sexually intimate with each other?

» What is one way you can deepen that connection this week and make it better?

» Do you feel hurt when you do not feel connected to me sexually?

» How do you feel when I am not in the mood to have sex and turn you down?

» What is stopping you from having sex with your spouse?

» Is sex just *sex* to you?

» Are you waiting for your spouse to change something so you can have great sex?

GET TO KNOW YOUR SPOUSE AND YOURSELF

How do you feel connected physically and sexually? Write down 5 ways with specific examples, so your spouse knows how best to connect with you. Then make it a point to do at least one thing your spouse listed every day.

Physically

Spouse A

1.

2.

3.

4.

5.

Spouse B

1.

2.

3.

4.

5.

<u>Sexually</u>

Spouse A

1.

2.

3.

4.

5.

Spouse B

1.

2.

3.

4.

5.

Chapter 7

FEAR OF INTIMACY

"Enlightenment is the key to everything, and it is the key to intimacy, because it is the goal of true authenticity."

– Marianne Williamson

Fear of intimacy, can be so subtle you don't even know you have it. Or, at least, you may not know there is a name for the struggles that you have when you try to be intimate with your spouse.

Do you put up walls to protect yourself with your spouse when you feel too vulnerable? Do you feel uneasy when feelings of closeness arise? Do you fear something bad is going to happen because good things in your life do not usually last?

Are you afraid of being controlled by your spouse, being rejected, or of losing yourself by getting too close? If you answered yes to any of those questions, then you may have a fear of intimacy, also known as intimacy anorexia. Most people are afraid to get hurt, but those with a fear of intimacy take it to another level.

They are scared to be vulnerable. They may start arguments when their partner is simply trying to discuss a difference in opinion, or even when things seem to be going well.

Someone who is afraid of intimacy will put up emotional walls when a relationship starts to feel too vulnerable. The truth is, that person may not even know he is doing it. *I didn't know I had this fear until I found a name for it. I knew I would have issues trusting a man and letting him get close to me because of my past. Growing up in an abusive home with a biological father who was repeatedly unfaithful and sexually crude towards me tainted my picture of men and my worldview for sure. I still didn't know that the lack of intimacy, closeness, and stability for most of my life meant I was starving for intimacy. Intimacy anorexia is really the best way to describe how I felt inside. The hole I had, never seemed to be replete no matter how I tried to fill it.*

When I met Marcus, I had a lot of walls up. My intentions were to have fun, take what I wanted and leave before I could be left. I was done giving of myself and leaving myself open to being hurt. I am still amazed at how fast we fell in love, and at how quickly I felt I could trust him. He is the perfect man for me, and he plowed through the walls I had erected. He asked me pointed questions from the beginning, wanted direct answers and he would not accept my sarcastic shrug-offs. (He actually never really understood sarcasm, and thought I was completely serious whenever I said anything.)

I remember having a phone conversation with a family member, gushing about how great he was, and this family member pointed out, "Ashley, you're falling in love." That was one of the scariest sentences I think I had ever heard. What? I can't be in love. It has only been a few weeks! I actually had a panic attack after that call when I realized that is exactly what was happening. I remember nearly hyperventilating in my car with my heart nearly beating out of my chest.

Why was this so scary to me? Why was I terrified? Because this man was close to me and he had the potential to do great harm. Because nothing good in my life had lasted long. Because my biological father would pretend he was cured of his addictions overnight, or after a few week's stint in rehab, and then things would get worse. After each high, the low would be lower.

This is the measurement I had for my life up until this point. To put it bluntly, I was scared shitless. – Ashley

CAUSES OF FEAR OF INTIMACY AND HOW IT AFFECTS YOUR MARRIAGE

Past experiences, fear of losing control, health issues like obsessive compulsive disorder (OCD), negative self-image, low self-esteem, infidelity from past relationships or parental influences can cause a person to be afraid of intimacy. Life experiences, lack of positive role models, or death of a loved one can also contribute to fear of intimacy.

Fear of intimacy can lead to pushing your spouse away subconsciously. It makes it difficult to express yourself fully to your spouse, and be vulnerable enough to build that true intimacy that a marriage needs. If you do not confront this fear and work through it, it can very likely lead to the end of your marriage. At best, your marriage will remain mediocre and much more superficial than you both have the potential to create. If you have a fear of intimacy, you could be unknowingly trying to sabotage your marriage.

Fear of intimacy impacts every area of your marriage, especially your emotional and sexual connection. Your spouse desires to be close to you and to know you as completely as possible. They may be able to let their guard down much easier than you. There is a risk of them seeking that connection elsewhere - intentionally or unintentionally - because you are not able to be open and connect with them.

How to Identify Fear of Intimacy

If you recognize you have trouble being totally open and intimate with your spouse, find out why. Is it a childhood experience, such as emotional, physical or sexual abuse? Lack of affection, low self-esteem, or past relationship experiences?

Could it be your family relationship history or experience? Are you able to love yourself? Are you afraid of trusting your spouse and the consequences of having that trust betrayed, or being rejected by them?

Is it uncomfortable to you when things feel good and you feel close to your spouse? Are you waiting for the other shoe to drop? Do you find it difficult to accept intimacy from your spouse? Are you worried about being hurt? Do you feel unworthy of love?

Do you push your spouse away emotionally or physically? Are you afraid of being controlled by your spouse? Are you afraid of losing yourself? Are you afraid that either your spouse or society wants to mold you into a different kind of person? These are all signs of fear of intimacy.

If you recognize any of these anxieties in yourself, it is important to take a deep breath and a step back. First, accept that you have this struggle. Find the root cause of this angst. Then, decide whether you want to move on and overcome this fear. Decide whether your marriage is worth the hard work and the difficult feelings that will come with overcoming your fears.

How to Overcome Fear of Intimacy

Make peace with your past. Recognize that the things that have happened were not your fault and were out of your control; but, what happens next is completely in your hands. You have full control over your life and choosing what future you want to live.

Next, slowly work your way to getting rid of the fear. Focus on the future for what could be. Do not dwell on feeling like you cannot solve this fear of intimacy issue. We highly recommend you get a professional to help. Find someone who can give you the tools, so you can help yourself move more efficiently through this difficult time. Again, just take baby steps.

Whenever I would get my feelings hurt in the beginning of our marriage (which was often because of my insecurities and low self-esteem), I would turn away from Marcus, walk away or just roll over, so I wasn't facing him. Facing him made it hurt worse. Rolling over was my way of building a wall of protection. Once I recognized this (with his help in pointing it out), I would force myself to roll back over and face him. That was the first step and actually really hard for me to do. It hurt me at first, a lot. Over time, it got easier and easier.

Doing this brought the opportunity to have open communication about what was upsetting me. I had to tell him I was hurt and why. By doing this, he would reassure me he did not mean something the way I took it, or that this was my emotion I had to take ownership of. These feelings were mine to work through. – Ashley

Another thing that can help you identify your triggers, is to write down your feelings when it happens and what transpired that day.

Accept that the fear of being intimate exists. Start sharing what you are afraid to share, and facing what you are anxious to face with your spouse. Learn to identify your fears of intimacy, why you may feel ashamed of yourself, why you may have feelings of anger, anxiety, depression, or mistrust.

Loosen your boundaries with your spouse by merging your lifestyle and existence while keeping your own identity. This can be a challenge for many couples to learn, but it is so worth it. Assimilating yourself with your spouse can be cause for much anxiety about losing yourself or feeling controlled.

Finding the balance of keeping your own identity will help ease those fears.

Practice managing your thoughts by replacing the fearful, doubtful, and negative ones with a more positive and reassuring thought process.

I would say to myself, "My husband is not intentionally trying to hurt me, let me ask him what he meant." Then I would tell Marcus, this is what I think you mean, or this is how what you said or did made me feel. Is this what you meant?

That way he knows how certain words or actions make me feel. It keeps that open communication going and I know his true intentions. – Ashley

Relaxing your boundaries enough to form a relationship identity with your spouse will not be easy. In fact, it will be extremely uncomfortable at times and scary. It is the direct opposite of what you have been trying to do all this time, which is building walls of protection and putting distance between yourself and the outside forces. You may have been hurt in the past and needed to create a fierce independence so that you never had to rely on another person. Either way, the task at hand may be daunting. I promise you, it is worth it.

Intimacy does not always have to mean losing yourself and your identity. You may be afraid that at your weakest moments your spouse may try to take advantage of you, hurt you, or abandon you. That insecurity is not the root of your anxiety, though. The real issue is your fear of not being strong enough to be able to relate intimately with your spouse or any other human being. You may fear that they will not be able to love you if they discover the real you; in essence that you are unlovable.

Brene Brown said it best, "Connection is what gives life meaning. The people who have a strong sense of love and belonging believe they're worthy of love and belonging. That's it. They believe they're worthy." So, find the balance of asserting yourself, your needs and opinions, while still respecting your spouse in the process. That is a healthy balance in a marriage. Emotions themselves are not good or bad; it is what we do with those emotions that can have positive or negative reactions.

One of the daily struggles I face is learning to love myself. This is especially hard when I feel as if I am not contributing, and in fact, taking from our relationship more than I should be. I have autoimmune diseases that affect my energy level and my physical abilities.

When I get fatigued and cannot get things done around the house, I know Marcus will be understanding and tell me to just try to relax as well as rest. He has said that to me so often. I am so thankful for his ability to be compassionate and understanding. I still have that guilt inside myself to battle.

I have learned to cut myself some slack and rest when I need to. I've learned not to push myself more than my body can tolerate. I have learned to look at myself in the mirror or pictures and not have a million negative thoughts. I have repeatedly retrained my thoughts to move from negative to positive.

I have learned to love myself through this process. I found that you cannot truly love someone until you love and accept yourself for who you are and appreciate your efforts to become better. – Ashley

Accept your imperfections and promise yourself (and your spouse when necessary) to do better next time. Learn to love yourself, one baby step at a time. This is the only way that you can truly love and be intimate with your spouse. Loving and accepting yourself is the only way you can properly feel love from your spouse. It is also the only way you will be able to trust that you are worthy of their affection and commitment. As a result, you will have a higher self-esteem too.

I can remember when we first started dating, I had a dream Marcus left me for another woman. I woke up mad at him and not trusting him, even though it was only a dream! This happened a second time, and I realized I was projecting my own expectations created by my biological father's infidelity onto Marcus.

Marcus was so undeserving of that mistrust and had done nothing to show me he was untrustworthy. That was something I had to work through. I had to retrain my brain whenever those thoughts and doubts came into my mind. He is a great man, and doesn't deserve to pay for the sins of my biological father. – Ashley

HOW TO HELP IF YOUR SPOUSE IS
AFRAID OF INTIMACY

Create a safe haven. Let your spouse know through your words and actions that you respect them, their boundaries, and that you are there for them. Let them know you love them and have no intention of hurting them. When you disagree, be sure to stay respectful and stick to finding a solution or compromise, not name calling, blaming, shaming, and other unhealthy fighting habits.

Learn to be vulnerable, even if your spouse is not able to meet you there at this time. Let your spouse know how much it means to you that they are making an effort to be close to you, and that you recognize their efforts. Verbalize to them that you understand this is not an easy task, but that you are there for them while they go through this struggle. Try to spend more time together even if it's doing simple little daily tasks.

Review your past history, and see if you have contributed to their lack of trust in you at all. If you have, apologize and commit to doing better. Work on communicating better. Communication with your spouse, connecting intellectually and emotionally, will encourage them that you desire their whole person, not just their body. Decide what boundaries you can draw around your marriage so that you both feel protected and able to trust each other.

Practice affectionate and non-sexual touching. Physical affection, as mentioned in the previous chapter, can help your spouse feel close to you and trust that you want to be near them, even when you do not want to have sex. Your spouse may need those extra touches to assure them that you are attracted to them physically. Physical touch could even be their love language.

Know when you need to give healthy critiques, and when to just listen.

Sometimes I got comfortable in between trying to work through this fear of intimacy. Having Marcus be honest with me and let me know when something was not working for him helped me stay focused on the task at hand and recognize other things I needed to work on.

He gently but firmly enforced his boundaries. This way, I was able to respect his limits and focus on the big picture of why I was working on bettering myself and working through this fear. He gave me the space I needed, the truth I needed (but didn't always want to hear), while still asserting his boundaries. – Ashley

Understand that your spouse may not be able to explain this struggle to you right away. The most important thing you can do is to create a safe environment for your spouse, and let them know you have their back.

A great example from Dr.Deborah Koshaba:

Take Jackie and Nick for example. When single, it was common for Nick to hang out with his friends several nights a week and well into the morning hours. Jackie was uncomfortable with this. Once Nick understood that Jackie wasn't trying to take away his freedom, he was receptive to change and establishing boundaries around this activity that satisfied both of them. Nick's understanding and receptivity went a long way to deepening the relationship and making Jackie feel secure.

(www.psychologyineverydaylife.net)

This is a great example of a couple who communicated their needs and made adjustments to their lifestyle that left both partners feeling respected and safe. Remember to be receptive when your spouse offers their feelings on your behaviors or habits. Try to see the underlying problem, and solve it together.

7 ESSENTIAL PILLARS FOR BUILDING A SAFE ENVIRONMENT

If you want to communicate your feelings to your spouse, or help your spouse overcome fears of intimacy, the first and most important thing you can do is to build a safe environment.

As you add each of the following 7 pillars to the foundation of your marriage, you and your spouse can erects a shelter both of you will run to in times of trouble.

Pillar 1: Be intentional.

In order to build a safe and peaceful environment for your marriage, make it a priority. Then commit to achieving this goal within the next thirty days. Talk to your spouse about why you really want to have a safe environment. Tell them you need their help so you can both create a safe haven for your marriage. Discuss and come up with a plan together to make your home safe for sharing your feelings, and being vulnerable with one another.

Pillar 2: Fear and Judgment Free

Is your spouse afraid of you? Are they uncomfortable around you? Does your presence intimidate them? Ask them, so you know if they are shy or anxious about your reaction and vice versa. Do they feel respected by you and you by them? Lack of respect and feeling like one has to walk on eggshells will hinder you from building a safe environment. In addition, don't judge your spouse. If they are afraid of being vulnerable to you, it's likely because they believe you will judge them or because of insecurities and baggage. No one likes to be judged.

Pillar 3: Learn how to communicate without fighting.

Considering most marriage problems couples face is due to the lack of effective communication or no real communication at all. We recommend you learn how to communicate effectively with each other. It's an essential skill for building that safe haven. When you are able to communicate effectively with your spouse, resentment goes away because you are able to resolve your marriage problems as it comes up. This is another reason why we recommend you schedule a minimum of thirty minutes to have deep conversations with each other every day. (An hour is best!) If you do not know where to start, then pick up our book, *Communication in Marriage: How to Communicate with Your Spouse Without Fighting.*

Pillar 4: If you are being a controlling spouse, stop.

No one wants to be controlled. Feeling controlled makes one feel uneasy and guarded. Imagine how you would feel if your parents tried to control you now. I'm sure everyone has felt that at one time or the other. It definitely did not make you want to comply. Would you want that to happen with your spouse? They tell you what to eat, where to work, who you can go out with, they choose your friends for you, they tell you what time to sleep, what time to put your kids to bed, how to parent your kids, how and when to wash the dishes or clean your house and how to dress.

A power struggle, manipulating, or lying and hiding things from each other, would become the norm in your marriage. When you are controlling, your spouse will not feel relaxed around you. They will be uncomfortable, which means the last place they would want to be is in your presence. If they are not in your presence, there is absolutely no way you can build that connection and intimacy you desire.

I *like control. I realize I can be a controlling person. I now know it is my way of keeping those I love and myself safe. I first realized I was doing this when I was a teenager. Since then I have been conscious of my controlling habits and broken them. I still need to check in from time to time with myself, but I have learned to let go. Letting go of that control has been really terrifying at times, but it always resulted in less stress for me as well as a sense of freedom.* – Ashley

Pillar 5: Listen empathetically and comfort.

Do not interrupt when your spouse responds to your concerns about the feelings you have. If you are not listening, you will not understand the feelings your spouse is trying to express and explain to you. As you listen, comfort your spouse, too. It's this warm and comforting experience of feeling empathized with and understood that you get from sharing your feelings that will help you to deal with the emotions you are going through.

Pillar 6: Start believing your spouse has the best intentions toward you.

You chose to marry your spouse because you knew they had your best interests at heart, and vice versa. If that's not the case, then why did you marry them? Why are they still married to you? Having a positive mindset about your spouse will reduce stress and diminish resentment in your marriage. Unless you are in a relationship where abuse of any kind is present, you must always remember your spouse has the best intentions towards you.

Pillar 7: Be very honest and sincere with your spouse, even when you think the truth may hurt.

We feel safest with someone we trust. Without trust, you cannot fully express and communicate your feelings to your spouse. You either do not trust your spouse will give you constructive feedback, or you fear your spouse may tell what you share with the world.

If trust is broken in your marriage, what can you both do to rebuild it? The sad truth is, until you rebuild trust in your marriage, having a safe environment for your marriage will not be completely possible. Trust is the glue that holds a marriage together. Work together to rebuild the trust you have for each other.

In order to openly share your feelings, you have to trust your spouse is not out to hurt you, but that they have the best intentions for you. You also have to feel safe with them and know that they will not broadcast what you shared with them to the whole world.

As humans, we enjoy doing things with the people we feel the safest with, whether that is sex, going on an adventure, or trying something new. The same applies to your marriage. Practice the 7 essential pillars, so you can make your home feel safe and primed for the connection you long for.

OTHER ROADBLOCKS TO INTIMACY

Is there a part of your marriage you can recognize that is creating roadblocks for intimacy? Now is the best time to start letting go of the things that prevent you from being intimately connected with your spouse. Could it be expectations you have for how your marriage should be? Or possibly certain people that have a negative influence on your marriage?

Maybe it is a habit that is hurting and not helping you or your marriage?

After being so starved of that intimacy for so long, once I found Marcus, I was really clingy. I always wanted to be close to him, always touching him. Looking back, I can see how he must have felt touched out, much like I do now with two young toddlers. If he ever said he didn't want to sit by me, or have sex, I would feel the ultimate rejection. But that was not him rejecting me; it was my insecurities I needed to work through.

I remember reading in a book somewhere that it helped to think of sex like pizza. Some nights you are in the mood for pizza, and other times, you prefer something else. That may sound absurd, but it helped me change my feelings of rejection into understanding by reminding myself that Marcus was just not in the mood for sex. It didn't mean he didn't love me or find me attractive. – Ashley

Being too clingy can be a put-off to your spouse and put a damper on them wanting to connect with you more. Be conscious of their needs for solitude, and make sure you are not overpowering them with your wants. If your spouse is the overly affectionate type and it overwhelms you, let them know how you feel. Be clear that you are not accusing or rejecting them. You are just expressing how you feel overwhelmed and want to find a solution that works for both of you.

Do you have anger or resentment toward your spouse that could be contributing to this disconnect in your marriage? In order to enjoy emotional intimacy with your spouse, you have to move through those emotions and take ownership of them. This is a personal issue that you need to deal with. Opening yourself up to your spouse, as you work through these tough feelings is integral to your success. You cannot receive intimacy and embedded connection from your spouse if you are unwilling to deal with your emotions of anger and resentment.

Are you able to love yourself? Are you overly concerned with your weight and appearance? Are you able to feel good about yourself? You won't experience true intimacy until you are able to truly accept yourself and all your imperfections. You will not be able to fully love your spouse until you learn to love yourself.

Being a woman who has struggled with my weight for as long as I can remember, I've suffered from low self-esteem. In fact, I don't believe I had very much self-esteem at all. But something clicked when I was around eighteen years old. I knew I had to love myself for who I was, accept myself for what I looked like. Years later, after getting married and having many insecurities come flying back in my face, I realized this self-esteem journey had a long way to go. I was not magically cured because I had found a man who loved me, as I had once naively thought.

After becoming a mother, I knew I did not want my girls to feel as negatively about themselves as I did growing up. I also knew they would follow what I did, more than what I said. I knew I had to model self-loving behavior. I vowed never to look in the mirror and say, "Uh! I look so ugly or fat." I looked for the positive, and things got easier. It is still a struggle, but it is getting easier every day. One thing I did was stop wearing as much makeup, and as often. I wanted my girls to see, that women do not need makeup to be beautiful. Makeup is fun for occasions, but no woman needs it.

After being diagnosed with an autoimmune disease, I had to ask myself the question, "Where am I attacking myself in life?" because "autoimmune" means my own immune system is attacking my organs. I realized again, I needed to work on my self-love. Since I started this, my life has improved drastically.

I've learned to forgive myself and to let myself relax when I need to rest. I've learned not to listen to that guilty voice in my head berating me for not doing the dishes or getting much done that day. If I don't love myself for who I am now and appreciate what progress I have made, I will never be happy. Happiness is a choice, and it has to come from within.

I choose to be happy. This was a choice I had to make for myself, but it will benefit my whole family. This is a daily challenge I take on, just as it must be for everyone. – Ashley

Robert Holden summed it up well, "Your relationship with yourself sets the tone for every other relationship you have." Body issues and lack of self-love are an emotional issue. Please seek the help of a professional counselor as they can help you have insight into where you may have a harder time on your own.

Fear of intimacy could be the sole reason why you do not feel connected to each other, so stop resisting and get to work on those baby steps. You chose to marry your spouse. What is holding you back from letting them truly know you, and you them? If you do not feel your spouse is a safe person, and they make no effort to become one, then you need to decide what is best for you, your happiness, and your emotional health. Having a counselor through this can help make this process more smooth and efficient.

Intimacy is not a one-way street. Unless both of you are open and emotionally naked with each other, true intimacy will not be possible. Intimacy is about committing yourself to one person, being vulnerable and trusting them. As Keith Miller put it, "Intimacy, as I am using it, is sharing my reality with you."

Chapter 8
KEEPING INTIMACY ALIVE

"There is nothing better on this earth than a soul you can connect with on every level."

– Unknown

Making sure you are connected to your spouse in every area of your marriage is integral to cultivating that lasting cumulative intimacy between the two of you. The first thing to do is have a marriage check-up. Find out where you stand in all the areas of your marriage that we mentioned. How fulfilled in your emotional intimacy and friendship do you feel on a scale of 1-10 this week? How about for your intellectual connection, spiritual, relational, social? How fulfilled in your physical intimacy and your sexual intimacy are you this week? What would make it better? What is one thing you both can do to make one of these areas a little better?

It is important to check-in as often as you can, and we recommend weekly, in addition to confronting any issues that come up during the week head on. These may be uncomfortable, awkward, and difficult conversations at first; but trust us, it will totally be worth it. If your spouse cannot read your mind, they don't know how you feel. If you don't open up then your marriage will not progress into a truly intimate experience.

Remember that being truly and intimately connected with your spouse is in your hands. According to Dr. Emma Seppala, "A sense of connection is internal: Researchers agree that the benefits of connection are actually linked to your subjective sense of connection" (www.psychologytoday.com). If you feel something is missing in your bond with your spouse, always look inward to see if there is something you need to do to change your situation first. It could be a mindset change, a new outlook, or simply something you have to ask your spouse to do or not do. You both have to be intentional about your marriage, or you will not have the ideal intimacy that we have explained.

Sometimes, you have to decide not to do something so you can have the time to connect with your spouse. For example, on special days like birthdays, anniversaries, and date days, we don't work on our business. By making this sacrifice, we are able to dedicate that extra time to our marriage. Yes, there is a lot to be done, but we cannot let those activities take over our marriage. You have to set your marriage as the priority. Do not give up on this opportunity to create this lasting and rooted connection with your spouse because you are hesitant to push past your insecurities and comfort levels. This type of intimacy does not happen by accident. Your marriage can always improve, and it will take effort on both of your parts.

If asking your spouse any of the questions we suggest in the book seems scary or impossible to you, ask yourself why. What are you afraid of them saying or doing? This may help give you some insight into issues you need to work on, or help you to bite the bullet and push past them. Make time to connect with each other every single day where you talk about more than work, kids, or the to-do list. Make time every single week for a check-in. Don't be afraid to rate the different areas of your marriage and ask yourselves (and each other) what you can each do to make it better.

This type of brutal honesty lets you both know where you each stand, and it lets each other know what you each need. However, your happiness and feeling that connection is your job as much as it is your spouse's to help you. Sometimes that "something is missing" feeling is something that you need to fix inside yourself. This is where mindset changes come in. Do you feel mentally healthy? Are you always looking for something to go wrong? Do you enjoy friction and always try to prove you are the one who is "right"? These are signs that some deeper-seated issues are going on within you. Looking inward and seeking a counselor to help guide you as you work through these issues will benefit yourself and your marriage.

Marriage can be a beautiful thing. If both spouses are truly committed, prioritize their relationship, grow independently as well as together, then they are on their way to creating a happy, lasting, and fulfilling marriage. It is all in your hands.

Think about the ideal marriage you want. Ask your spouse what theirs is, and then make a plan to create that marriage.

As you have read from Ashley's example, lack of intimacy between married couples affects the children in the relationship as well. Putting in the extra effort it takes to build true intimacy in a marriage will not only benefit the couple but also their children in a trickle down affect.

Take the steps in the areas of your relationship that need improving. Learn how to communicate effectively with each other. If you do not learn how to communicate effectively with each other, you will stay stuck and most likely have unmet needs. Strengthen your marriage in every area with baby steps. Work on yourself, work on your communication, and try to grow together.

To truly connect with your spouse, you first have to forgive them for the past. If you resent your spouse, you will find it very difficult to reconnect with them. We talked about things to help build trust between you both like complete honesty, laughing together, and communication. Before your spouse can connect with you, they must feel safe and secure with you. How do you do this? By being honest and sincere with each other. Put yourself in your spouse's shoes. It may be difficult, but it will give you a different perspective. Would you be happy if your spouse was not providing or meeting your intimacy needs after you expressed explicitly what you needed?

Be compassionate with your spouse. If your spouse feels connected to you, they will be in a better place to listen and work with you; so, this is a win-win for both of you. You are on the same team. You will either both be winners, or both be losers. When you choose to create intimacy in your marriage, you are changing your mindset. If you don't believe your marriage is worth putting in all this hard work and choose to stay guarded, then you will not achieve the intimacy you crave. It is as simple as that. We have given you the tools you need to get to work on enhancing intimacy in your marriage, but now it is up to you to decide which outlook you will choose today, tomorrow, and every day after that.

We believe the ideas we have mentioned in this book can help you strengthen your intimacy individually, together, and even if you are apart due to deployment or overseas. If you are trying to reconnect after having a baby, deployment, or separation, start with baby steps. Relax, and work on your communication first. Empathetic listening will play a huge role. Try to get to know each other and enjoy each other's company. Work on clearing the hindrances you come across when giving your best efforts to build intimacy.

A lot of people think intimacy is just about the sexual aspect of your marriage. They don't realize it has to do with all these areas of connectedness. In order to find out how you and your spouse feel the most united, you have to have a conversation and continue that exchange throughout your marriage. Check-in every week with your spouse, and work on having both of your connection measuring cups as full as possible.

Protect the intimacy you have created in your marriage. A simple way to do this is to not put down or disrespect each other in private or in front of others. Do not over share about your sex life, or anything that your spouse would be uncomfortable knowing you shared it with others. Set up boundaries and safeguards within and around your marriage. Schedule time to connect every single day, even in the midst of chaos. One hour a day is best. If you feel like you have nothing to talk about, you can think of questions to ask each other.

Another way to protect the intimacy you both have worked so hard to create is not to play games with each other. Do not expect your spouse to read your mind. If you feel emotionally distant from your spouse, let them know. Do not try to lose weight or wear something sexy to get their attention without letting them know what's going on. If they don't notice, then this can backfire on you. Be open about how you feel and where you need more connection and how you need it. Honesty is the best policy.

5 THINGS WE DO EVERY DAY TO STRENGTHEN INTIMACY

"We are what we repeatedly do. Excellence, then, is not an act, but a habit."

– Aristotle

If you truly want to strengthen intimacy in your marriage, then you have to do something every day that will help you achieve this goal. In our case, it was connecting every day. Over time, the results have been amazing. You can do the same for your marriage. You can even apply the same principle to other areas of your marriage like communicating effectively, respecting each other, and being patient.

We have done the five things listed below for such a long time they are now part of our daily life.

1. Spend a minimum of thirty minutes talking with each other.

2. Give each other long hugs and kisses.

3. Check-in with each other when one is away and when we are together again.

4. Say *I love you* and mean it, multiple times a day. Say it in different ways: in person, by text message, or via phone call.

5. Say *thank you* and mean it in multiple ways. Say it in different ways: in person, by text message, or via phone call.

What's more, we have created two intimacy challenges for you to use to start reconnecting with your spouse, a 30-day and a 12-month challenge. So take the first baby step, and choose to start this intimacy challenge. We have given you the tools for your intimacy toolbox, and now it is in both of your hands. Choose each other every day. When you make mistakes, apologize and promise to do better next time; then, do just that.

QUESTIONS TO ASK YOURSELF AND YOUR SPOUSE

» What does intimacy mean to you and your spouse?

» How do you each feel intimately connected to each other?

» Write down ten ways you each feel loved. I feel loved when you...

» Write down ten ways you each feel connected to each other.

» Do you see any similarities?

THE 30-DAY & 12-MONTH INTIMACY CHALLENGE FOR COUPLES

Thank you for reading our book. Because we want to help you and your spouse apply what you have learned from this book in your marriage, we have created a 2-in-1 intimacy challenge for you.

This intimacy challenge is so simple that you can do it whenever you want to connect or reconnect, strengthen, and improve intimacy in your marriage. It is designed as a 2-in-1 format so you can see positive results within the first thirty days of successfully doing it.

The first intimacy challenge involves doing a 30-day challenge with your spouse. The second intimacy challenge involves completing a 12-month challenge that coincides with the thirty-day challenge so you can truly connect with your spouse and strengthen intimacy in your marriage.

First, write down why you both want to do this challenge on a sheet of paper or in the intimacy worksheet, which you can download at www.ourpeacefulfamily.com/intimacy-worksheet. What goals do you want to achieve at the end? Keep this written information somewhere because you will need to revisit it at the end of each challenge.

Second, complete the 30-day challenge. Once you are done with it, spend the next day discussing how you feel about doing the 12-month challenge with your spouse. What did you like or not like about the 30-day challenge? What went right or wrong? What impact did it have on you, your spouse, and your marriage? What would you change in the future?

After the discussion, begin the 12-month intimacy challenge. We have a pre-planned list for each month that you can follow. However, feel free to change to activities that suit your lifestyle and marriage. The activities for each month must not be repeated within the twelve-month period.

Now let's get started.

30-Day Intimacy Challenge

Length: Thirty consecutive days.

To Do: Spend quality time (thirty minutes at least) engaged in meaningful conversations every single day. *An hour is best.* Make use of the questions we have listed in this book to help you delve deeper and get to know each other more intimately.

The goal for this challenge is about communicating and building a safe haven. We want you to focus on one single thing: spending time to have deeper, meaningful, and thought-provoking conversations together.

Why?

Because communication is the best foundation to build intimacy, connect and reconnect with your spouse.

In addition to communicating every day, fill each day with an action to help you both feel connected to each other in different ways.

Remember you both wrote five things that make you feel connected with your spouse for each chapter? Now each of you should pick your top fifteen ways and write them down.

You will end up with a list of thirty ways to connect with each other, which will be used for your 30-day intimacy challenge.

Your list will look like this:

Day 1: Spouse A's answer

Day 2: Spouse B's answer

Day 3: Spouse A's answer

Day 4: Spouse B's answer

And so on for thirty days.

For each of the thirty days, you should both focus on doing what you have written on your list for each other. Even if you do not feel connected that way, your spouse does. You could also follow the 30-day challenge we have created in this section if you do not want to use your lists.

If your spouse is not receptive to attempting the challenge, ask them how they feel connected to you and focus on doing that for thirty days. In the beginning, your spouse might not be interested, but over time, they will gradually start to feel connected to you and will want to return the favor because of the law of reciprocity. This law basically means that humans feel obliged to give back upon receiving. The overall goal is to enhance the intimacy of your marriage and that will require both of you working towards this goal together.

If you do not want to use your list, here is one we put together for you to do for each of the thirty days:

Day 1 Do something thoughtful for your spouse.

Day 2 Kiss hello and goodbye to your spouse before either one of you leaves the house for work, errands, good morning and good night, etc.

Day 3 Tell your spouse you love them while making eye contact. List a few specific reasons why you love them so much.

Day 4 Surprise your spouse with one of his or her favorite inexpensive things. For example, you could make his coffee or bring her breakfast in bed.

Day 5 Dance to your wedding song and reminisce over your wedding photos, scrapbook, or album.

Day 6 Be vulnerable and open up to each other. Share your struggles and challenges about intimacy and connecting with each other.

Day 7 Show your affection to your spouse in their love language. (Don't know what your love language is? Take the free quiz at www.5lovelanguages.com).

Day 8 Send your spouse flirty text messages throughout the day.

Day 9 Have spontaneous sex. It doesn't matter who initiates, or what time it happens.

Day 10 Do a workout or exercise together. It could even be meditation or yoga.

Day 11 Talk about your faith and spiritual journey.

Day 12 Be vulnerable and open up to each other. Share your struggles and challenges about life, your career, and dreams.

Day 13 Do something to show your spouse you cherish and appreciate them.

Day 14 Go to bed naked together.

Day 15 Go for a walk together, even if it's just around the block.

Day 16 Have a twenty-second hug and kiss.

Day 17 Draw or paint a picture together. Pick an activity that requires both of you to collaborate.

Day 18 Make out without the expectation of sex.

Day 19 Work side-by-side on your personal hobbies. You can also read side-by-side.

Day 20 Do one of your spouse's chores for them.

Day 21 Whisper I love you into your spouse's ears when they least expect it.

Day 22 Pray together.

Day 23 Give each other one of these above the waist physical connecting activities: a back rub, massage, kissing, or snuggling. Do this for a minimum of five minutes.

Day 24 Add a new flavor to your sex life. Try something new and different to spice up your sexual intimacy. For example, have sex in a different room of your house, try a new sex position, mix up your foreplay, act out a fantasy, or add in a sex toy.

Day 25 Write "I Love You" somewhere your spouse will see it, like a notepad, bathroom mirror, or car window.

Day 26 Tell your spouse you believe in him or her via text, in person, email, or phone call.

Day 27 Talk about your financial plans, where you are today, where you want to be in three years, and create a plan on how to get there together.

Day 28 Be vulnerable and open up to each other. Share your struggles and challenges about sex.

Day 29 Be vulnerable and open up to each other. Share your struggles and challenges about communication in your marriage.

Day 30 Dream together. Talk about your hopes and dreams, what you want to accomplish as individuals, as a married couple, and as parents. What kind of marriage do you want in five years? Twenty years? Make a plan to get there together. In addition, make a time capsule to open a year or five years from today.

To further enhance your 30-day intimacy challenge:

» Ask your spouse his or her opinion about something that has been on your mind within the last thirty days.

» Pursue and flirt with your spouse like when you first met.

» Tell your spouse one thing you need the most from him or her.

» Be there for your spouse.

From our experience, we know a demanding job, kids, a side business, and other responsibilities will make it difficult to have intimate conversations every day - unless you schedule it. So, schedule a minimum of thirty minutes to talk with each other every single day. For us, it's usually between thirty to ninety minutes in the evening after we get our children to bed. It may not be easy, but just being able to have meaningful conversations for at least thirty minutes with your spouse every day will *transform* your marriage.

If you miss a day, find out what prevented you from making your appointment with each other so you can avoid that mistake again. Obviously, emergencies happen, kids get sick, and some nights you will be exhausted and need to go to bed early. Just make sure it doesn't become a habit, and your connection time is the priority. By completing the challenge for each day, you and your spouse will be able to build upon your conversations from previous days.

Furthermore, pay attention to each other during this period because your undivided attention is required for a meaningful conversation. These conversations can lead to so many wonderful things like amazing sex, and deeper connection. To help you have better conversations, check out the list of questions in the various chapters, plus the conversation-starter questions in chapter two.

This 30-day challenge will help you to start connecting in different ways. The daily check-in, thank you, random hugs and kisses, sleeping or cuddling naked, laughter, flirting, etc. are added bonuses for this challenge. However, that should not be your focus, because this 30-day challenge is more about talking just like you did when you first met. Having conversations that are meaningful make you fall more in love and come to know each other intimately.

Remember to discuss the progress you made with this challenge before you start the 12-month challenge.

12-MONTH INTIMACY CHALLENGE

Length: 12 Months.

To Do: Write down 12 activities you can do together over the next 12 months.

This 12-month challenge is intended to build upon the 30-day challenge. The goal for this challenge is to have a monthly *intimacy activity* to do together as a couple, similar to monthly date nights.

You and your spouse must choose, plan, and schedule twelve intimacy activities that you can do together as a couple for the next 12 months. Below is a 12-month pre-planned schedule you can use. Feel free to modify it to suit your interests and lifestyle.

January - Learn about each other's love language at www.5lovelanguages.com and discuss your results. In addition, show affection to your spouse using their love language every day for this month.

February - Make it a game night. Play a board, card, or dice game. (Visit www.ourpeacefulfamily.com/games to see over ninety games for couples, from sex games to fun and family games.)

March - Go watch a movie, sports game, show, live event together, and display your affection publicly.

April - 7 Days of sex challenge. If you need more information on how to complete this challenge, check out the book *7 Days of Sex Challenge* by our good friends Tony and Alisa DiLorenzo.

May - Volunteer together.

June - Cook or grill out together.

July - Watch a sunrise or sunset together.

August - Read and discuss one book together

September - Attend a sip and paint class.

October - Plan a get away for a few hours, days, or a whole weekend.

November - Write a thank you note for your spouse every day for this month. At the end of the month, conclude with a love letter.

December - Plan for the next year, set goals together as a couple, and choose one book to read together.

That's it! This 2-in-1 intimacy challenge gets easier when you do it consistently. You can also use this challenge as your intimacy lifestyle for your marriage. And don't forget to write down your experience in a journal to serve as a memory.

Other intimacy activity ideas for the 12-month challenge:

» Kiss your spouse when you wake up every morning this month.

» Learn the basics of a foreign language together.

» Learn about a new culture, country, or society.

» Create a game together. You can even try to improve one of the board, card or dice games you have.

Now, visit www.ourpeacefulfamily.com/intimacyworksheet to get your copy of the free fill-in-the-blanks printable PDF for this challenge.

As always, you can find us at: www.ourpeacefulfamily.com.

THANK YOU

Congratulations on reading our book! We are very thankful and excited to help you connect or reconnect with your spouse.

If you enjoyed reading this book, please leave us a review on Amazon and share the book with other couples. We would both love to know how this book impacts you and your marriage and what we can do to make it better.

You can also send us an email about any questions you have about intimacy in marriage to firstyearmarriage@gmail.com.

We cannot promise that we will immediately reply every email due to the volume of emails we receive, but we will do our best to cover your question in future blog posts or podcast episodes.

If you would like to receive email updates about future books, courses, and more, visit our website today to join our book fan community: www.ourpeacefulfamily.com/bookfan.

Thank you again for choosing and reading our book!

Marcus and Ashley Kusi

Enjoy your marriage, enjoy your life!

OTHER BOOKS BY MARCUS AND ASHLEY

» Communication in Marriage: How to Communicate with Your Spouse Without Fighting.

» First Year of Marriage: The Newlywed's Guide to Building a Strong Foundation and Adjusting to Married Life.

» My Tandem Nursing Journey: Breastfeeding Through Pregnancy, Labor, Nursing Aversion and Beyond.

RESOURCES

If you have not yet read the books below, we highly recommend you get a copy from your local library or buy one online.

1. The Five Love Languages by Dr. Gary Smalley.

2. Love and Respect by Dr. Emerson Eggerichs.

3. Boundaries In Marriage by Dr. Henry Cloud.

4. The Total Money Makeover by Dave Ramsey.

5. QBQ: The Question Behind The Question by John Miller.

6. 7 Days of Sex Challenge: How to Rock Your Sex Life and Your Marriage by Tony and Alisa DiLorenzo.

7. Communication in Marriage: How to Communicate with Your Spouse Without Fighting by Ashley & Marcus Kusi.

You should also check out the list of excellent marriage resources we recommend for couples by visiting our website below:

» www.ourpeacefulfamily.com/resources

» Listen to the *First Year Marriage Show* podcast (www.firstyearmarriage.com) to learn from the first year marriage experiences of other amazing couples.

Links to resources about spiritual sexual connection

» www.mindbodygreen.com/0-12737/why-sex-should-be-treated-as-a-spiritual-practice.html

» www.hiddenmysteries.org/spirit/ecstacy/reclaiming.shtml

» www.christianpost.com/news/look-where-the-soul-goes-during-sex-81046/

» www.health-science-spirit.com/spiritualsex.html

» www.thespiritscience.net/2015/09/28/taking-love-to-the-next-level-the-secret-to-an-oxytocin-intimate-connection/

» www.lonerwolf.com/transforming-sexual-energy/

» www.earthconnections.wordpress.com/2014/05/03/sexual-energy-and-spiritual-energy-2/

REFERENCES

Cook, Gareth. "Why We Are Wired to Connect." *Scientific American*. N.p., 22 Oct. 2013. Web. 17 July 2016.

Cacioppo, John T., Ph.D. "It's Time for a Science of Social Connection." Psychology Today. N.p., 16 July 2010. Web. 17 July 2016.

Seppala, Emma M., Pd.D. "Connect To Thrive." Psychology Today. N.p., 26 Aug. 2012. Web. 17 July 2016.

Parker-Pope, Tara. "The Happy Marriage Is the 'Me' Marriage." The New York Times. The New York Times, 31 Dec. 2010. Web. 10 Aug. 2016.

Khoshaba, D. (2011, November 4). Fear of Intimacy: Are you a relationship saboteur? Retrieved December 04, 2016, from http://www.psychologyineverydaylife.net/2011/11/04/fear-of-intimacy-are-you-a-relationship-saboteur/

"Divorce Statistics." Information on Divorce Rate Statistics. Web. 18 May 2016.

ABOUT MARCUS AND ASHLEY

We help overwhelmed newlyweds adjust to married life and inspire married couples to improve their marriage so they can become better husbands and wives.

We do this by using our own marriage experience, gleaning wisdom from other married couples, and sharing what works for us through our website and marriage podcast, *The First Year Marriage Show.*

Visit the website below to listen to the podcast.

www.firstyearmarriage.com

Visit our website to learn more about us.

www.ourpeacefulfamily.com

Marriage is a life-long journey that thrives on love, commitment, trust, respect, communication, patience, and companionship. – Ashley and Marcus Kusi

Made in the USA
Columbia, SC
23 February 2018